DESTINAT. ᴝN HIRED

THE DEFINITIVE GUIDE TO GRADUATE SCHEME & TRAINING CONTRACT APPLICATIONS

ZACHARY REDSMITH

CAREERSGEEK

"I dedicate this moment, to all the people who believe, that the biggest dreams, can still come true".

Bret Hart

CONTENTS

SPECIAL BONUS

See the back of this book for a free **special bonus** I hope will benefit you greatly in your graduate scheme and training contract applications.

TERMINOLOGY: TRAINING CONTRACTS OR GRAD SCHEMES?

For ease of reference, throughout this book both graduate schemes and training contracts are referred to under the collective term **'grad scheme'** (a training contract is a type of graduate scheme). The techniques, methods, hints and tips in the **Application Success** section are all relevant and apply equally whether you are applying for graduate schemes, training contracts, summer vacation schemes ('vac schemes') or internships. Any specific differences are called out and discussed individually as they arise.

FOREWORD

It's been quite a few years since I began my grad scheme at one of the world's leading management consultancies and professional services firms, working at the very top of the 'Big Four' auditors. And honestly, it changed my life. I've worked with some of the best consultants and professional services personnel in the world, on cutting-edge projects at FTSE 100 companies across the UK and Europe, including personally leading projects at two of the Big Four banks here in the UK.

From very early on in my career, I got involved in my company's graduate and experienced hire recruitment, in addition to my day-to-day responsibilities as a management consultant. Later, I became responsible for leading our recruitment at one of the top London universities (University College London). I also led the recruitment process in my department for experienced hire joiners.

But before all of that happened, I was a graduate, looking at starting my first application process, and with no idea how to do it. I quickly discovered that the graduate application process can be a long and very complex road without the proper guidance. It took quite a while to find the right resources to use, and longer to identify what grad scheme recruiters are really looking for. I discovered that grad scheme applications are a topic in their own right; a topic that needs proper preparation, time and attention if you want to be successful.

This book is the one I wish I had had all those years ago, when I was starting out on my own application journey. It brings together all of the information you will need to succeed in your graduate applications. It is also the product not only of what I learnt in my own application process, but also the expertise I gained from actually working as a recruiter for one of the world's leading consultancy firms, in addition to insights from my day job of being a management consultant and project manager.

In writing this, I hope to make the path to graduate scheme and training contract success easier and more accessible for you. I believe that if you are resourceful enough to seek out this book, and to put the time in to implement the lessons you can learn from it, you should have every chance of succeeding and gaining the opportunity of a great career in future. This book won't do the work for you, but it will tell you *how* to get onto a grad scheme: how to find the right scheme for you, how to tackle each part of the application process, including the Assessment Centre and interviews, and finally, what to do at offer stage.

Graduate schemes and training contracts are wonderful things. They give you all of the training you'll need to get started in your future profession, while giving you a great personal and professional network of colleagues and the opportunity to work at the height of your industry, and all of this while getting paid a great salary at the same time. In short, they will give you the best possible start to your working life. Buying this book and following the steps in it represent an investment in your future. The first step to achieving that future starts now.

Zachary Redsmith

HOW TO USE THIS BOOK

Whether you are well underway with your applications and need help on a particular stage of the process, are about to get started, or aren't sure where to begin, this book is here to act as your guide through your application journey. If you are already underway with your applications, or need help with a particular stage in the process, you can skip ahead to the sections most relevant for you right now (though if you do that, be sure to read the **'Application Skills Toolbox'**, since this has vital information and strategies for succeeding which we will refer back to throughout the book).

This guide is organised as follows:

- **Part 1** introduces the preliminaries you will need in place to succeed in your applications. It works through the 3 First Principles you will need before getting started. The Application Skills Toolbox is essential reading that will benefit you throughout your applications.

- **Part 2** contains everything you will need to succeed through each stage of your application journey. It gives you a detailed, end-to-end, guide through the application process for graduate schemes and training contracts, covering all the different phases through application forms, psychometric tests, Assessment Centre tasks, and the various kinds of interview.

- **Part 3** looks at what to do at offer stage, what happens when you receive an offer, how to choose the right offer for you, and what to do when you have competing offers. We also look at what to do if you don't receive an offer, before finally looking at how you can hit the ground running and get started in the best way possible when you start at your new employer.

PART I

GETTING STARTED

1 FIRST PRINCIPLES

Welcome to Destination Hired. This book will serve as your comprehensive guide throughout the application process for graduate schemes and training contracts (hence referred to collectively as 'grad schemes'). Buying this book is a great sign that you take your applications seriously. Taking it seriously is one of the 'first principles' which you will need in place before you get started in order to be successful in your applications.

Imagine you're about to go on holiday. There are a few fundamental things you need to do before you set off: you need to research destinations, hotels and flights, you need to book tickets, and lastly you need to pack your bags. It's no different for grad scheme applications. Without having done the preliminaries, you'll be lost at sea, with no idea of how to navigate and without the proper knowledge or skills to see you through testing waters.

Make no mistake: grad scheme applications are difficult. They are hard work and take effort, because they are meant to test you. Grad scheme employers are usually world class and give you the best possible start to your working life.

They provide all of the necessary training, skills and knowledge to set you off towards having a thriving, long and successful career. In return for that, they want only the best. So the applications process is rigorous and there is immense competition for places.

However, if you equip yourself with all of the strategies, knowledge and skills you need beforehand, and if you have all of the first principles and a framework in place before you get started, not only will you not get lost at sea, but you'll steadily progress through each stage of the application journey towards your final destination of getting an offer. Yes, it will be difficult, and it will take effort, but this book is here to help you and it will show you the way. Now all you have to do is set your course and keep going until you get there!

Principles

At this stage, if you haven't already done so, I strongly recommend you pick-up and read my **free** book *The Framework: Everything you need to know BEFORE applying for Graduate Schemes and Training Contracts.* It's absolutely free of charge and will walk you through the fundamentals you need before making your applications. See the back of this book for how you can get your copy. **However**, in case you are pressed for time, below is a summary of the fundamentals you'll need in place and why you need them:

Principle One: Know Your Motivation

This is probably the most important principle, for two reasons:

1. At every stage of the application process employers will test your motivation. They want people who are driven, motivated and passionate, not just about getting onto a scheme, but about working in their industry, working in the role they're offering, and working specifically for them - not any out of a bunch of other employers. More on this later.
2. You need the motivation to see you through the rigorous application process. Applications are purposely difficult. This book will equip you with the knowledge you need and hopefully inspire you too, but you'll need your own motivation to provide the metaphorical wind in your sails to power you through.

To get motivated, you need to know your reasons for doing a grad scheme. This boils down to knowing the pros and cons of schemes and fully buying into the positives of doing one.

The positives of grad schemes include working for an industry leader in your chosen profession, having excellent training, the chance to attain industry-respected professional qualifications and certifications (for some industries, this includes gaining accreditation with your profession's governing body in order to practice, such as seeking admission to the Roll of Solicitors at the Law Society in order to become qualified and attain your first practising certificate as a solicitor, for example), opportunities to travel, a dedicated support network of both more senior colleagues and peers, and the chance to work alongside and learn from some of the best professionals in your field.

You will get paid a great salary on a grad scheme, one far above the national average; however, this cannot be your only motivation for doing one. Not only will this not impress recruiters and interviewers, but it just simply isn't enough motivation to carry you through the rigorous demands of a grad scheme. A surprising number of candidates quit their schemes early despite the great salary. You need to really be passionate and *want* to be there. For a full discussion of pros and cons please see Section 2 of *The Framework*.

Principle Two: Have Your Shortlist Ready

Some candidates mistakenly assume that the more grad schemes they apply to, the more chance they'll have of being successful. In fact, almost the exact opposite is true. Because each employer's application process is designed to test you, each application requires finesse and quality. This means that the more applications you rush through in the time you have before the deadlines, the less chance you'll have of creating quality applications. You'll likely get rejected. Too many candidates make this mistake.

To give yourself the best possible chance of success in your applications you need to be *selective* about which employers you apply to. This doesn't mean that you should only do one or two applications, however: you need to hedge your bets and have a few in the pipeline in case any of them fall through for whatever reason. **The optimal number of applications to do is between five and ten**, at least in the first batch. This gives you the time you need to do all of the employer research you need and to craft a **quality** application tailored to that particular employer (more on this in Section 3.1 Getting Organised).

Principle 3: Have a Mindset for Success

You could have the first two principles in place, all of the necessary credentials, talent and qualifications to get onto a great scheme, plus all of the talent in the world and still fail to get an offer. Mindset is the crucial difference factor between success and failure. It is different to motivation in that motivation is temporary unless it is translated into action. Mindset is the attitude you bring that will translate your motivation into action. The two critical components you will need are:

- **Perseverance:** Once you have all the knowledge and skills in place for tackling each stage of the application process, plus the other two first principles, the

7

difference between success and failure lies in **consistent effort** and in **not giving up**. Perseverance is the combination of these two things. It means applying yourself - your skills and talents plus the knowledge you will gain from this book. Keep going in your applications and don't stop until you have an offer of a grad scheme from a great employer on the table. Thomas Edison said, "Our greatest weakness lies in giving up. The most certain way to succeed is always to try just one more time".

- **Patience:** Perseverance and effort are crucial, but they have to be *sustainable.* You can start your application journey with a large amount of energy and make it through the initial assessment stages, only to stagnate in the middle stages.You also need to take the time to build in quality in everything you do. This means that *patient* perseverance is the approach you want to take - working consistently and diligently at your applications, steadily progressing to offer stage. Having energy is good, but pace yourself for the duration of the application process and avoid rushing.

2 NAVIGATING THE APPLICATION PROCESS

Each grad scheme has a slightly different application process. The steps are largely similar, but tend to appear in different orders depending on the employer. The rest of this book contains the essence of your journey through the graduate applications process. We will work through all of the good practices, strategies and approaches for success through the various stages. Each section is designed so you can dip in and out, choosing what is relevant for you.

The diagram on the next page shows the core components of a typical application process. The more you prepare in advance for each stage by using the knowledge from the relevant section, the better prepared you will be to pass the stage successfully.

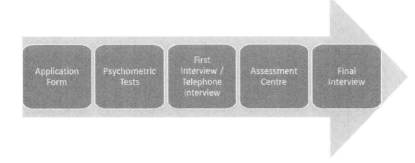

Depending on the employers you apply to, not all of these components may appear, or they may appear in a different order. Choose how you progress through the rest of the book based on what is relevant for you in regard to the application process you are currently working through. It is highly recommended to read Section 3 Application Skills Toolbox, however, since it contains essential strategies for success that will apply throughout all of the stages, and we will refer to these strategies throughout the rest of the book.

Note: It is typical to have an early stage interview at some point in the process. This tends to be a competency-based interview, although strengths-based interviews are gaining in popularity. Since many of the interview strategies apply across all types of interview, rather than confuse the structuring of the book, the sections relating to different types of interview are grouped together in Section 7 Interviews. Should you have a first-stage interview of this type, skip ahead to that section accordingly, before coming back to look at Assessment Centres.

3 APPLICATION SKILLS TOOLBOX

3.1 GETTING ORGANISED

Keeping track of all of your applications and research is absolutely fundamental to your success. Once you get underway with the process and have multiple applications running at the same time, it'll be easy to lose track of which one is which. You can easily mix up which employer offers that lucrative signing bonus versus which one offers you more flexible benefits, and so on.

In an ideal world, you would work through an entire application process from the initial form all the way to final interview for one employer at a time. In that way, you could keep all of the research and information for different employers clear in your mind without confusion. But in reality, submission deadlines mean that as soon as you send one form off, you should start work on the next.

Once you get started, you'll quickly end up at different application stages for different grad schemes. You'll be juggling doing psychometric tests for one, with preparing for a case study interview for another. It's vital that you keep your employer research compartmentalised, both in your mind and in how you do your research. Few things are worse at interview than giving details about the wrong employer in response to a question. Your interviewer will take it as a sign that you haven't done your research properly, which means you aren't passionate about working for them, and they will reject you. This applies at all stages of the process, from the application form all the way through to final interview. Here are three very effective ways of organising your applications:

1. **Physical notes:** Buy an A4 ring binder with dividers. Create a divider for each grad scheme you apply to and store any printouts and handwritten notes for each employer in its own divider section. It's a good idea to create a summary page at the front of the binder. Add a table to it to update with which stage you are at in the process as you progress through each application. Think of it like an active table of contents.

2. **Spreadsheet:** Use Microsoft Excel. You don't need to be a spreadsheet wizard or particularly proficient at Excel to do this. Just use the tabs at the bottom left of the screen in the same way you would use physical dividers. Create a tab for each employer and paste in any links relevant to your research in each relevant tab. You can also type your own notes directly into the

Excel sheet in each tab. It would be a good idea to dedicate your first tab to being a summary sheet as we saw with the divider method. Here you can create a table listing the status of each application for the employers you have applied to, and also keep track of what actions you need to take.

3. **Soft-copy folder structure:** The third method is to create a logical folder structure on your PC, laptop or Mac. You then store relevant bits of research in the appropriate folder. Label the main folder 'Grad Scheme Applications' or 'Training Contract Applications'. Then, within that folder, create a subfolder for each employer you are applying to and store all relevant information and notes in these per each employer.

Remember that these are suggestions only. If you have another method that works better for you, then use it. The important thing to remember is that preparing for grad scheme and training contract applications is like preparing for an exam. You'll need to keep your notes on each employer separate so you don't confuse any of the information, in the same way you would keep your notes separate for different modules and exams.

3.2 TWO CRITICAL STEPS

There are two critical steps you need to take before starting any application if you want to succeed. These two steps will need to be repeated for each of the employers in your shortlist that you apply to.

Step 1 - Research, research, and more research

You've chosen the first employer on your list you want to apply to. Recruiters there will be looking to test your knowledge about them as an employer, about their grad scheme, and the role they are offering you. They will test your knowledge of this in different ways throughout the process.

One of the fastest and surest ways of ruling yourself out of the running is to not do your research. The reason for this is that employers only want to recruit people who are passionate about working for them, and doing the kind of work that they do, while being afforded the opportunities that they offer. A passionate employee is not only a productive employee, but one who is willing to go the extra mile to deliver quality, because they are passionate about the work. Only someone who has done all of their research can really become passionate about what the employer and their grad scheme offers.

There are three fundamental things to research for each employer you apply to. We look at this in depth in 3.5 Three Key Questions, but to introduce them here, they are:

- **The employer itself:** what is their history, how are they positioned in the market, how are they structured and where does the department you are applying for fit within that structure? What are their strengths and weaknesses, who are their clients and competitors, what are their products and services?

- **The grad scheme** (in case you didn't research this in Part 1, or even if you did, you should refresh your knowledge now): how long is the scheme, what training and qualifications are offered, will there be variety and rotation involved between types of role and departments?

- **The role:** what exactly will you be doing day-to-day (after you complete the initial induction and training process), what will your responsibilities be, what type of tasks will you be doing, what does a typical day look like, how much travel will be involved?

There is a fourth thing that you should also research, in addition to the Three Key Questions, and this is the employer's competencies. We will look at this at length in the next Section 3.3 Competency-Based Applications.

You will need to know each of the above points thoroughly to make it through the process and be made an offer. The side benefit of doing this research is that you'll be able to confirm for yourself whether this organisation sounds like the kind of employer you want to work for.

This will save you valuable time and effort. If you do somehow manage to make it through the rigorous application process without completing your employer research first, you might still quit a few months into the job, if you later realise this employer isn't a good fit for you.

One of the best resources to help in your research is an employer's own graduate recruitment website (or the graduate recruitment section of their main site if they don't have a separate site). These pages will have been written by their grad rec team, the same people who wrote the application form and who will be assessing you throughout most of your application process. For any employer you apply to, aim to be as familiar with their recruitment material as possible.

Another good option for your research is to pay a visit to your local or university careers services. They may have promotional recruitment leaflets and brochures from the employers you are applying for or their competitors.

Do an online search for recent news articles involving the employers you are applying for as well. Being up to date with their latest developments is a great way to show you are passionate about working for them. Be careful with news articles though. Every employer gets its share of bad press. Try to avoid discussing anything at interview and during your applications which might show this employer in a negative light.

Step 2 - Go meet them!

There is no substitute for going out and meeting the employer. It'll help inform your knowledge on everything from the type of people that work there and the work that they do, to the organisational culture and whether you'll fit in.

It'll also impress at interview to say, "I was really interested to hear about Project x / Client y when I came to the presentation at the graduate recruitment event last month, could you tell me a little more about the type of work you do with them please?". This shows you were motivated enough to go out and attend their recruitment events and have taken an interest in what was said there.

Employers often list upcoming graduate recruitment events on the recruitment pages of their websites. Also make sure to check out any careers fairs local to you and check with your own university's careers service for scheduled events; many graduate scheme recruiters will actively target university campuses.

Make sure that you research events as early as possible, you don't want to miss out because you were late finding out about an event. Keep track of upcoming events in your notes.

3.3 COMPETENCY-BASED APPLICATIONS

Almost all application processes for grad schemes are *competency-based*. If you want to succeed in your applications, you're going to need to find out all about competencies, including what they are, how they differ between different graduate employers in your industry, and how to go about answering competency based questions.

Graduate recruiters and interviewers are unlikely to use the word 'competency' with you, since this tends to be a term that is used by people who work in the recruitment industry. However, you can assume that you will be evaluated according to competency criteria (even if you do not have to sit a formal competency-based interview). This is because competencies are the most effective way to assess what transferable skills a graduate candidate has. Because of this, competencies are relevant throughout every stage of your application process.

What are competencies?

Competencies are a set of transferable skills that recruiters look for in a potential joiner. They differ slightly between different employers, but a good list of common competencies across all graduate jobs includes:

- Team-working skills;
- Commercial awareness;
- Problem solving and lateral thinking;
- Communication skills;
- Presentation skills;
- Ability to prioritise; and
- Time management.

This is not an exhaustive list. Each employer will have their own specific competencies that are built into the culture of their organisation. They want to recruit people that are the right fit for their organisation, and the best way for them to do this is to test that applicants have the competencies they are looking for.

Why are competencies used for graduates and not experienced hires?

Competencies are a great way for employers to assess whether graduates have the skills they're looking for. It wouldn't really be fair, or practical, for employers to assess graduates in the same way that they do experienced hire applicants who have been working for years in their field. An experienced hire applicant would have to answer experience-based questions about the roles they have had in the past, and possibly a technical interview or assessment as well. These types of assessment are not applicable for graduates, since graduates will not have yet had the chance to gain the experience or technical skills required.

Instead, employers use competencies to identify the transferable skills they look for in a graduate joiner. Once on the grad scheme, the employer will provide training and expertise in order to flesh out these skills with valuable industry knowledge.

Since competencies are transferable skills, they can be evidenced in other ways outside of work. You can use examples from academics, sports and hobbies, charity work and volunteering, and other interests.

The key thing to realise with competencies is that employers are looking to see that you have the core skills they are looking for. They are not looking for you to be the finished product, in the same way that an experienced hire with several years of experience working in that industry would be. Instead, graduate employers are looking for people with the skills they value; they will then use their grad scheme to provide you with the necessary skills, knowledge and experience to *become* an experienced professional in your field.

Identifying an employer's competencies

You can find out a graduate employer's competencies from their recruitment website and promotional materials. Though they won't be described as 'competencies', you'll find sections telling you about the skills they look for in applicants.

Keep an eye out for mention of skills like **team working** and **communication**. You can identify additional skills by reading through their recruitment material. There will often be content about the role itself (such as 'a day in the life of a trainee solicitor'), see if you can spot the type of skills required to do the job. Maybe problem solving, or strong presentation skills are relevant. Perhaps client interaction plays a regular role, and so having strong people skills is key.

The graduate recruitment material that an employer produces is a fundamental resource for finding out about them. Try to know this material as thoroughly as you can. It will help you when it comes to answering wider application and interview questions, as well as identifying the competencies.

We'll return to look at competencies and how you can answer competency-based questions using the STAR method in 7.2.1 Competency-Based Interview. For now, it's enough to know that graduate recruiters at the employers you apply to will be looking for evidence that you meet their competency framework. Know what their competencies are, and see if you can come up with a list of examples that show you have demonstrated those competencies through your life experiences.

3.4 COMMERCIAL AWARENESS

Commercial awareness is the ability to understand the economic context in which an employer operates. This will include knowing something about the wider market for an industry, the main players in the market, what the major products and services are, and so on. For those applying for grad schemes in the financial services sector and closely related industries, it may also involve understanding and using financial terms. However, the degree to which you need to be commercially aware will depend on the employer and industry.

For those applying for grad schemes in the financial sector, or a secondary service provider to the financial sector, you will need a greater degree of commercial awareness. In this case, that would be any applicants for banking and insurance, financial advisory, law, accountancy and audit, and any other financial services related company. This doesn't mean that if you aren't applying for any of these industries that you don't need to be commercially aware. Employers expect all graduate joiners to have the relevant degree of commercial awareness. But the extent to which you need to know and understand the terminology will vary.

The good news when it comes to commercial awareness and grad scheme applications, is that it is not usually tested during the early parts of the process. This gives you some more time to brush up if you haven't already done so. The bad news, is that it takes time to develop commercial awareness. Think of commercial awareness as being more like a skill that you develop over time, rather than simple knowledge you can acquire. The earlier you start, the more you will be commercially aware. Paying attention to market trends, following publications to do with your industry, subscribing to e-mail newsletters and listening to relevant podcasts are all great ways to develop relevant commercial awareness over time.

Acquiring commercial awareness

The following are all great sources for developing commercial awareness:

- Pay regular attention to the financial press, particularly for your industry: this doesn't mean you need to read the Financial Times every day, but it does mean that you should keep a close eye on what is going on in the market, what the general trends are, and what the major players are doing.

- Subscribe to newsfeeds and mailing lists: setting up an e-mail alert can be a great way to get regular market updates.

- Podcasts: have a look out for industry specific podcasts; some large employers even have their own. There is an excellent podcast from BBC Radio 5 Live called *Wake Up To Money.* Listening to this every day will go a long way to developing great commercial awareness over a few weeks or months.

- Join societies and clubs: attend relevant university society events to do with your industry, finance or economics to help keep you up to date with market and industry news.

- Internships and vacation schemes: these are a great way to boost your commercial knowledge by actually working in the field you are applying to, or a closely related one.

- Part-time jobs: similar to internships and vacation schemes, showing that you have worked for a small business and understand the flow of money and wider considerations in transactions is a good way to gain commercial awareness.

Demonstrating commercial awareness

Commercial awareness will usually be tested at the interview stage of an application process. If you have developed good commercial awareness, it will reflect in your answer to questions. Don't think to yourself, "This is a commercial awareness question, therefore I have to pack in as much financial terminology and industry knowledge as possible".

Instead, let the knowledge you have gained over time naturally speak for itself. If you can talk with confidence about the market trends, latest developments and competitor movements of the employer you are interviewing for, you will have demonstrated good commercial awayness skills in a convincing and natural way.

A bad answer would be talking about *how* you have acquired commercial awareness **only** e.g. by saying, "I read the Financial Times every day". Instead, you need to show that you *understand* the commercial context in which the employer operates.

3.5 THREE KEY QUESTIONS

I f you take nothing else away from this book, make sure you learn this section. It is crucial to succeeding, not just at grad scheme interviews, but for any type of interview you'll face beyond graduate level as well. There are three fundamental questions that you will **always** be asked during any job application process. No reputable employer will make you an offer of employment unless you have answered these three questions successfully. And nowhere is this more relevant than in grad scheme applications, where these questions will be asked more than once, and often in several different ways, throughout your application process.

Although you will be asked a number of different questions during your applications and interviews, if you fail to provide a good enough answer to any *one* of these three, you will not be made an offer. The wording of the question might be slightly different, they might ask you them in a roundabout way, but ultimately you *will* be asked these three questions, because they are fundamental to an employer's decision-making process about whether or not to hire you. It is, therefore, crucial to succeeding in your applications that you learn what these questions are, and how to go about answering them.

Question 1: Why do you want to work for us? (Why us?)

Variations of this question include: "What makes us stand out from our competitors?", "why do you specifically want to work for this firm" and, "what excites you about the possibility of working for us?". With this type of question, the interviewer wants to know two things:

- **That you have done your research into their organisation:** One thing interviewers hate to see is a candidate who has not thoroughly done their research into what they are about as an organisation. It wastes the interviewer's time, because there is no way they will offer a role to someone who has not taken the time to find out anything about the employer they are applying to join, regardless of how good the candidate is on paper or what their qualifications are. The interviewer will also check that your answer is specific to this *particular* employer and their grad scheme. They will know instantly if you are giving a generic answer that could apply to any of their competitors.

- **That you are *passionate* about working for this employer:** Employers want to hire passionate people, not someone who would be happy to simply go through the motions of the job, without really caring about what they are doing or producing quality work. In other words they want to root out people who are just treating this as a pay cheque, and not as a career. Employers want to hire people who care about the quality of their work and the level of service provided to clients. A passionate employee is someone who is emotionally invested in doing a good job, and will often go the extra mile to make sure that there is quality behind everything they put their name to (and, by extension, the employer's name as well). This emotional investment only comes when you know what the employer's vision and strategy is, have bought into it and are passionate about it. Someone who has not done their research into the employer cannot be someone who is also passionate about working there.

Answering Question 1

There are two key elements to satisfactorily answering this question. The first is to have thoroughly done your research into this employer. You need to know everything about what makes this organisation unique, in terms of the products and services they provide, but also in terms the details of their grad scheme. You need to show why you specifically want to work for *them* and not their competitors (even though they know you will very likely have also applied for their competitors).

If you don't think there is much difference between this organisation and any of their competitors in the market then you have not researched thoroughly enough. No matter how close two or more employers look, there will be unique differences in their strategy, client base, culture, history and group values.

You will find these differences among even close competitor organisations, including the Magic Circle law firms, the Big Four accountancy and consulting firms, and among any other closely matched group of employers. If you are applying for a public sector grad scheme and there are no competitors as such, the interviewers will still want to see that you have done your research; this is because of the second element of answering question 1.

The second part of answering this question is around showing that you are *passionate* about working for this employer. You might have been thorough in your research and you might be saying all of the right things, but unless you are enthusiastic in *how* you answer, it will not be good enough.

The interviewers and assessors want to see that you are *excited* about the prospect of working for them. This essentially comes down to the *energy* you bring to your answer, if you are animated, in both the way you speak and your body language, this will communicate to the interviewer that you are excited to be there.

This doesn't mean that you should be frantic or over-zealous, but it does mean that you need to do enough to show your interviewers and assessors that you are interested in what you are saying and that you are excited about the prospect of working there.

Practise answering the 'why us?' question to friends or family, and ask for their feedback on whether you look and sound like someone who is genuinely excited by the prospect of working for this employer. Think about how you feel when you discuss something you are really interested in with a friend, like a hobby or your favourite TV show; how do you behave when you talk about it? See if you can bring the same level of interest and engagement to your answers when you practise this question.

Question 2: why have you applied for this role/job/grad scheme? (Why this role?)

Variations of this question include, "What attracts you to this type of job?", "What do you think a typical day is like in this role?", "Give me an example of what typical tasks you expect to do during your first year and what excites you about that", and, "Which parts of our grad scheme would you most look forward to and why?".

With this question, the interviewer wants to find out how much you know about the *job itself*. This is different to the first question, where you are being asked about knowledge of the employer. This time they want to see that you know what's involved in the job on a day-to-day basis. They want to see that you know what your tasks and responsibilities will be, and that you know what a typical day looks like.

Again, there are two reasons they ask this question at interview. The reasons look similar to those for Question 1, but there are very important differences. This time, the interviewer will want to know:

- **That you have researched the demands of the job:** The interviewer wants to see that you know what the everyday realities of the job are, and that you are prepared to meet those realities. Things like regular travel, long hours, any studying required and qualifications they will expect you to complete, and so on. They will also want to see that you know the typical tasks you will be asked to perform as part of this role.

- **That you are passionate about this *role:*** For the same reasons we saw with Question 1, the employer will want to hire people who are passionate about their work, because people who are passionate will care about the quality of their work. This time, however, the interviewer will want to see that you are passionate about the *job itself,* not just the employer. You might be quite passionate and emotionally invested in working for an employer, but when it comes down to it, you might not be very passionate at all about that specific job or role. You might dislike the actual day-to-day realities of the job, and the kind of tasks involved. Perhaps you love the idea of working in management consulting, for example, but you find the prospect of regular travel and unpredictable hours and working locations less appealing.

Answering Question 2

Every graduate employer will have a section on their main website detailing what the requirements are for the role you are applying for. Sometimes these sections take the form of 'a day in the life of one of our graduates'. Some employers' websites are more detailed than others.

The good news is that graduate-level roles tend to be very similar among competitor organisations who are similarly placed in the same industry. This means that you can get a good idea of what type of tasks are involved in the role you are applying for by looking not only at the website of the organisation you are applying for in this instance, but also at their closest competitors' websites.

The best way, however, of getting good information on what types of tasks are involved in a graduate role for an organisation is to go to their graduate recruitment events or to careers fairs and meet them. Employers often send people from their graduate joiners to represent them at recruitment events. By attending these events and asking questions about the role not only will you get a great view of what the requirements and realities of the role are, but also what type of people the organisation employs. In other words, you'll find out about the culture of the organisation and whether you're a good fit for that culture or not, as well as getting the information you are looking for around the day-to-day role.

When it comes to giving an answer to this question during an interview or assessment, just like with Question 1, a good answer relies both on showing that you have done your research into this *specific* role and grad scheme, and that you are passionate about it.

Question 3: Why should we hire you? (Why you?)

Variations on this include, "What do you think would make you effective in this role if we hired you?", "What skills and experiences make you particularly suited to this role?" and, 'What differentiates you from other candidates?".

This question is about testing that you can match up your transferable skills and experience to the requirements of the job and skills sought by the employer. They are looking for you to join up your own transferable skills with your answer to Question 2 (why this role?).

Occasionally interviewers will combine Question 2 with this one, by just asking you this one. In other words, they might ask "Why should we hire you?", without having first asked about your understanding of the job. If that is the case, the interviewer will be expecting you to answer both questions in your answer. You will need to demonstrate your awareness of the tasks and responsibilities involved in the job, as well as matching these types of tasks up with your own skillset.

Refer back to our chapter on Competency-Based Applications and also see the chapter on Competency-Based Interviews for how to successfully answer this question.

3.6 THE JOB TO GET THE JOB

Completing grad scheme applications is usually an involved, demanding process, one that takes discipline, good organisation skills, patience and perseverance. The best way to get an offer on a grad scheme, to get the job as it were, is **to treat the application process itself like a job.**

To be successful at your applications you'll need to be organised with your time and consistent in your effort. Let's look at ways to do this:

- **Schedule a time for applications:** Schedule a time every day to do your applications. Try to make this the same time every day. The human mind likes familiarity: the quickest way to get into the groove of doing applications and get past any pre-application anxiety is to build a habit around doing them every day.

That means consistency in your approach. Find a time that works best for you and stick to it until it's part of your daily habit to sit down and do applications at that time. Once you've done this for a few days, you'll start to build **momentum**, and it'll get easier and easier for you to sit down and work on your applications.

- **Pick the time when you're most productive:** Some of us work better in the morning and others late at night. Either way, find the time when you are at your most productive and have the least distractions. Most productive means that you should be at your most alert and least tired (without the use of caffeine).

- **Prioritise your application time:** There are always distractions in life from any task. But when we are faced with something new that looks a bit daunting, it's easy to procrastinate and create additional distractions for ourselves to put off doing what we need to do. Time is a valuable commodity and particularly valuable for your applications. Give yourself every possible chance at succeeding by short-circuiting these distractions. Try putting your phone on plane mode or switch it off during the time you are working on your applications. Stay off social media and YouTube as well. Make sure family or flatmates know not to disturb you during this slot, or find somewhere to work where you know you won't be disturbed.

- **Chip away one day at a time:** Don't be tempted to rush through each application form: a rushed form will just get rejected. Although you should be mindful of your application deadlines, it's far better and more productive to chip away at the form than to rush it. Break it down into sections and tackle each section one step at a time. This also applies for every step through your application journey, from doing employer research all the way to final interview.

- **Get started!** Sometimes we can trick ourselves into not working by thinking we are being productive through doing endless research. This 'analysis paralysis' is our mind trying to trick us into avoiding facing the anxiety of starting something new (in this case your graduate applications). The hardest part of any task is getting started. Once you've done that, half the battle is already won. After you've completed your preliminary research into the industry, the employer, their grad scheme and read Section 3 Application Skills Toolbox and Section 4 Application Forms, you should get started. Open up your first form and begin filling in the personal details section. You will return to this book to prepare for each subsequent stage of the application process, so don't put off starting your first form any longer than you need to and get started!

PART II

APPLICATION SUCCESS

4 APPLICATION FORMS

Although it's usually the first step in the process, the application form can be one of the hardest. Recruiters come across thousands of application forms every year and are looking for ways to quickly eliminate the ones that don't meet their standards and expectations.

With so much competition for places, recruiters will first scan through a form and eliminate it from the list if they find basic errors. Any forms with generic answers, or where it's clear that the candidate hasn't done their research, are the next to go. They'll also eliminate any forms where the answers waffle and are not concise.

The following points might sound straightforward, but you would be surprised how many candidates fall at this hurdle. Don't be caught out by any of the following:

- **Spelling, punctuation and grammar:** although this sounds basic, putting the time in to properly check and proofread your form before you submit it will tell recruiters that you mean business, that you have carefully crafted your application form and that you care about working for them. If there are spelling mistakes, typos and grammatical errors, it will look like you have rushed through this application among a raft of others, and that it's just a numbers game for you. Take the time to properly check through all of your answers several times before submitting.

- **Business language:** this doesn't mean financial vernacular, it means conciseness and brevity. Keeping your sentences short. The application form is a good way for recruiters to assess your written communication skills. Business language is all about conveying your message in as concise and simple a way as possible. When you're at work, you won't have time to read through lots of lengthy e-mails. They look to recruit candidates who have the same mindset. Avoid elaborate wording and lengthy sentences. It may sound counterintuitive, since you want to answer in as much detail as possible, but putting across your answer in a concise way is what they are looking for. This doesn't actually mean providing any less detail; it means getting that same content across in a direct, simple and straightforward way. Many graduates fall down during this part of the application process because they answer the questions as if they are writing an academic essay. But this really is a case of less is more. If, for example, on an application form it asks you to list five reasons why you want to work for this employer, a bullet point list of five responses will do fine. Some forms help you keep your answers short by having word or character limits for each answer (usually 200 or 300 words).

- **Employer-specific examples:** this is where all of your research will come in. Employers will be sure to ask you why you want to work specifically for *them*. Successful answers will come across as being passionate about the type of work they do, wanting the skills gained from the training provided on their grad scheme, being fascinated by their big cases or projects, and being excited about potentially working with their client base and why. This shows that you have taken the time to thoroughly research the employer you are applying for, that you know what they're about and want to work for them. It also shows that you care about quality in your application and have taken the time to tailor it to that specific employer.

Structure of the application form

Application forms are usually hosted on an online portal that allows you to save your progress as you work through the form. The beginning sections will usually be short answer questions about your personal details like home address and contact information, and your education details such as A-Level and degree results. There will then be a section for long-answer questions, asking you to go into more depth.

Avoid using an unprofessional e-mail address. Something like ThaGr8st@gmail.com is just not appropriate for this and they are not likely to take your application seriously. Instead use something simple with your full first name and last name like John.Bloggs@gmail.com or Jane.Bloggs27@gmail.com.

Make sure you only include correct information, particularly for your academic information, qualifications and references. Many employers use fact-checking agencies to carry out background due diligence checks after a candidate accepts a job offer. Professional and ethical integrity is incredibly important to employers, and they will not be impressed with any applicant trying to put forward false credentials.

Some forms will ask you to attach a CV or covering letter to the online form itself. If you are asked to provide a CV, make sure it is no more than two pages long, has only accurate information about you, and is written in as concise a way as possible. Covering letters should also be brief, not more than one page and using concise language.

Tips for completing the form

- **Take your time:** give each form the relevant time and attention it needs. You should expect to spend at least a full day on each form, including research and drafting all of your answers. Take your time to make sure everything is completed with the right level of detail needed.

- **Save regularly:** application portals have been known to crash, make sure you save your work as you progress through each stage of the form and at regular intervals. Avoid the mistake of clicking 'submit' instead of 'save'.

- **Draft your answers elsewhere:** it's useful to draft your answers outside the form (in Microsoft Word for example) and then paste them in when you are ready. Word processors have spell and grammar checking, and can provide character and word count. It will also feel less pressurised to draft your response outside the main form; you'll avoid the pitfall of having to write the 'perfect answer' on your first draft. Instead, work on it somewhere else and only paste it in when you are happy with it.

- **Read the questions carefully and more than once:** there is nothing worse than spending hours drafting a response to the wrong question. Make sure you read through all of the application form questions very carefully before you begin to draft a response. Plan your responses before you come to write them. Try putting together a bulleted list of all the points you want to get across in your answer. Then start your first draft.

- **Deadlines:** always make sure you are aware of the deadline for your particular application and that you are well in advance of it. Do not leave your form until the last minute. Not only will it make it rushed, but the likelihood is that all of the available places may have been filled already. Although graduate recruiters leave a window open for when they will accept applications, in reality it will be first come, first served. Once they have filled all of their positions, they will not read your form, even if the system allows you to submit it.

- **Tailor your responses:** make sure that your answers are specific to the employer you are applying for. Include references to things that are unique to that particular employer, the type of deals, projects or cases they have worked on, their client base, their place in the industry, the specific training they offer, their charity and community outreach programmes. Recruiters will quickly spot generic and regurgitated responses and will eliminate them. But also be mindful of just copying across the material they have on their recruitment website. You have to make your responses personal to you, in other words, what excites you about a particular employer's client base, grad scheme or training opportunities, and why?

- **Check through your form thoroughly:** before you submit your form, print it off and review all of your responses. Make sure every question has a response, that your spelling, punctuation and grammar are correct, and that all personal and academic details are correct. Also make sure that you have spelt the employer's name correctly and have avoided incorrectly including examples from other employers (it has been known for some applicants to misspell the name of the employer they are applying for. Some have also mistakenly included the wrong research by talking about a competitor instead. This is why it's so important to keep your research organised).

- **Take a copy:** save a copy of your form. If you get invited to interview, you will want to know your form off by heart. The interviewer will always have read your form; they may even have a copy of it with them in the interview and ask you to elaborate on some of your answers.

- **Hit submit:** once you've thoroughly checked through the form and are happy with all of your answers, then **submit it**. Don't wait around thinking you'll perfect it or let nerves get the better of you. Submit it and congratulate yourself on tackling the first hurdle

Once you've submitted your form you will usually get an auto-mated e-mail saying it has been received. It can take anything from a couple of days up to a couple of weeks or more to get a response. Now is the time to get started on another application: don't wait around putting all your hopes on one employer. Assuming you make it through to the next stage for this partic-ular application process, you will still want other applications in the pipeline to hedge your bets in case this one falls through at a later stage in the process for whatever reason.

5 PSYCHOMETRIC TESTS

Psychometric tests (sometimes called aptitude tests) are often used in the early stages of the recruitment process for large graduate employers. They are usually held online, meaning you can do them remotely from home, under timed conditions. Depending on the employer and industry involved, the tests can consist of numerical reasoning, verbal reasoning, personality tests and situational awareness tests. Some employers will include psychometric testing as part of an in-person Assessment Centre; however, the approach to preparation and success with these is the same.

Some candidates find this stage particularly daunting, especially if you are faced with a numerical reasoning test and do not have a numerical academic background. It is not uncommon for some candidates to have done very little to no mathematics since GCSE. This should not be a problem. Every year, candidates from all types of non-numerical backgrounds receive grad scheme offers from employers, even in industries known to particularly value numeracy skills. We will look at some of the different types of psychometric tests and what you can do to prepare for them, and then look at some resources to help you in your preparation.

Three-step approach

How difficult or easy you find psychometric testing depends entirely on how much preparation and practice you do before-hand. The amount of practice you do is really the key to succeeding at psychometric tests. Once you've identified the tests involved, it's a matter of brushing up your skills and repeatedly doing practice tests until they become second nature and you score a high passing mark **every time**.

1. **Identify the tests:** find out the type of tests you will be asked to sit (you will usually be told this in the invitation to a test, but the employer's graduate recruitment website should tell you, or you can also phone their recruitment team and ask). Will there only be numerical and verbal reasoning, or are there tests on logical reasoning, personality and situational awareness as well?

2. **Refresh your knowledge:** Once you know the type of test, brush up the skills required for this type of test (more on this in the next section).

3. **Do practice questions:** Once you know the type of tests you will be given, and you have brushed up on the skills required, it's time to do practice questions. Lots of them. Practise over and over under timed conditions until you consistently score a percentage in the high eighties or nineties. These tests are usually very time-pressured, so practising getting the questions right under timed conditions is vital.

Types of psychometric test

Numerical Reasoning: this is designed to examine a candidate's basic numeracy. The level of mathematical ability is no higher than that needed for GCSE maths. Do not underestimate the test, however: it is still highly time-pressured and the multiple choice questions are designed to try to confuse you.

A good tip is to have a look at some GCSE study guides (the CGP books are a great resource for this, see if you can get hold of a copy of the CGP GCSE guidebook for mathematics) and refresh your knowledge of the four topics listed on the next page.

These four topics are the ones that come up in numeracy psychometric tests. Learn any formulae needed (such as how to calculate percentage change) and then do practise numeracy psychometric questions until you feel confident. You will also need the ability to interpret data from simple graphs and tables; practising questions will also help with this.

- Basic calculations (addition, subtraction, multiplication, division)
- Percentages (including calculating percentage change)
- Probabilities
- Ratios

Verbal Reasoning: textual analysis, the assimilation and interpretation of written information, is a large part of most graduate jobs. Verbal reasoning questions will present you with a paragraph of text to read, and then you have to answer a number of multiple choice questions about its meaning.

It might be tempting to assume this is going to be easy, particularly if you have studied a degree involving a lot of textual analysis and reading. But don't underestimate this type of assessment. There is a particular knack to answering these questions, and just as we saw with numerical reasoning, the more you practise, the better. The assessment is testing not just that you can read a block of text, but *how you think.*

Some of the answers can be very nuanced. At first glance, the correct answer might seem obvious, but take your time and consider all options before you click through to the next question. The correct answer might not be as obvious as you first think. They are not asking you to answer with an everyday interpretation of the text, what you would usually think outside the assessment context. Instead, they are examining your *logical interpretation* of the text. So you'll need to consider each multiple choice answer carefully before you select it. The wording can have a very different logical meaning than you would mean in everyday speaking. Imagine you're talking to a computer that will interpret everything you say literally. The more you practise these types of question and have a look at the answers, the more you will get a knack for working out what they are looking for.

Personality Tests: there is little you can do to prepare for personality tests. In any case, it is better to answer these types of tests truthfully rather than second-guess the type of personality they are looking for. The employer wants to know if you are a good fit for them, but it's also a good opportunity for you to find out if they are a good fit for *you.* Answering truthfully based on your actual personality and not getting the job, is better than to go as far as getting the job and then eventually quitting because you and the employer are not a good match

Other Tests: some employers will offer other types of test, including technical tests for engineering and IT applicants, logical (deductive and inductive) tests, situational awareness, and tailor-made tests created by the employer themselves. These latter types can sometimes be presented as a game format, looking to test how calm you are under pressure, your reaction times and spatial awareness. As with all types of exam, if you apply the three-stage approach we've looked at, you will be prepared to pass. Graduate employers will sometimes put practice tests on their recruitment pages. If you have access to a practice test then repeat it over and over until you feel confident in passing. Do not limit yourself to just this one practice test, however; try as many different ones as you can.

Strategy for psychometric tests

- **Practise:** The number of practice questions you do is directly proportional to your chances of succeeding in the real test. The most important thing to passing this stage of the application process is repeating your practice tests over and over. Do not be discouraged if you get a low score when you first start out: many candidates experience this. Once you've spent a few days going through practice questions you'll quickly start to hit the pass marks. Persevere with your practice until you regularly score a percentage in the high eighties or nineties.

- **Practise under *timed conditions:* p**sychometric tests are designed to be **very** time-pressured. Do all of your practice tests under timed conditions until you get in the habit of finishing the test with a high pass mark within the allotted time.

- **Use the elimination method:** psychometric tests are almost always multiple choice. Even if you feel confident that you know the correct answer, you should use the elimination method. Multiple choice answers can appear very similar and without considering all of the options you may not be selecting the correct answer. For verbal reasoning tests, sometimes several answers are partially true, but the correct one is the one that is 'more right' than the others. To use the elimination method, work your way through the multiple choice options, ruling out the ones you are confident are incorrect, then keep eliminating answers you believe to be incorrect until you arrive at your final answer.

- **Do not underestimate the test:** this is a stage in the application process like any other. Failure to succeed at this step will mean your application with this employer will not progress. Don't do yourself a disservice by not taking the tests seriously and not preparing enough. Psychometric tests are easy to pass provided you put the time in to repeatedly practise under timed conditions. Use the resources we will look at next to brush up your knowledge and repeatedly practise until you are confident for the real thing.

Resources for psychometric testing:

Books:

There are some highly useful books on psychometric testing, and most of them contain practice tests with model answers. Many libraries stock books on psychometric testing in their careers and personal development sections. Check with your local library to see what they have in stock.

A good series of books is the 'Brilliant Psychometric Test' series:

- *Brilliant Passing Numerical Reasoning Tests* published by Pearson. ISBN: 978-1292015415

- *Brilliant Passing Verbal Reasoning Tests* published by Pearson. ISBN: 978-1292015453

Online practice tests:

The following links provide free practice tests:

- Psychometric tests from SHL, including practice tests for verbal reasoning, numerical reasoning, inductive reasoning, accuracy and motivation: http://www.cebglobal.com/shldirect/en-us/practice-tests/

- A large collection of test links is available on the website of Business Psychologist Dr. Mark Parkinson: http://www.markparkinson.co.uk/psychometric_links.htm

- Several practice tests are available on the Saville Consulting website: http://www.savilleconsulting.com/PracticeTests

- Numerical reasoning and critical thinking practice tests from TalentLens (UK), Pearson: http://www.talentlens.co.uk/practice-aptitude

6 ASSESSMENT CENTRES

Assessment Centres follow on from the initial stages of an application process. They are usually held at the employer's offices, although sometimes can be at an external venue, and can last anywhere from half a day to a full day. Expect somewhere between five and twenty other applicants to also attend. Some employers schedule final interviews for the same day (depending on a candidate's performance during the assessments), though many also schedule these at a later date.

The day is comprised of a number of different assessment tasks. Although these vary between employers, they are likely to include: **e-tray assessments, written exercises, case studies, presentations, group exercises and interviews.**

Find out what tasks are involved in your upcoming Assessment Centre (either from the invitation, the employer's recruitment site, or by phoning their grad recruitment department). Once you know the tasks, prepare carefully using the material from the relevant sections of this book.

6.1 PREPARING FOR ASSESSMENT CENTRE

Assessment Centres can look quite daunting. At first glance, it seems like you are being invited to a day-long exam with a group of other candidates who are all competing with you for the same job. Having a mindset like this will only hinder your performance and reduce your chances of doing well on the day.

The truth is that there is never just *one* job up for grabs at an Assessment Centre. I have seen *no* offers being made at Assessment Centre since none of the candidates on that particular day performed well, and I've also seen four or five offers being made from the same Assessment Centre. Don't assume that they will definitely progress one candidate, or that it will be *just* one candidate that they will progress; it entirely depends on performance on the day. The kind of employers that offer grad schemes usually do not have quotas for each individual Assessment Centre. They would also prefer not to turn down quality candidates. This means that if you are good enough on the day, the chances are that they will progress you to the next round.

A mindset geared towards succeeding at the Assessment Centre stage will consist of the following elements:

Collaborative, not competitive

To succeed at Assessment Centre, you should focus on your *own* performance. Don't compare yourself to how you think the other candidates are doing: this will only serve to stress you out. In reality, no matter how confident someone else might appear, they might not actually be scoring well with the assessors.

Trying to compete with the other candidates will also work against you, because the assessors are looking to hire **team players**, not people who do not work well in a group.

In the television show *The Apprentice*, the candidates always compete with each other in a cut-throat way to win the task. This is precisely the opposite of what real recruiters are looking for, or how to really operate in the business world for that matter.

The assessors are looking to hire people they can see themselves working *with*. Being collaborative, while still influencing others and standing out due to your performance is the behaviour they look for.

Pace yourself for the long run

Endurance and stamina are key factors during Assessment Centres. The day is meant to test you, not just in the individual tasks you will face, but also the cumulative effect the day has on you. If you are tense and stressed, you will quickly feel drained and run out of energy. The body is not meant to sustain high levels of stress or adrenaline for prolonged periods of time.

Inevitably, you will face some stress, particularly before the Assessment Centre starts and perhaps during the first task. But once the day is underway, try to settle into a calm state of mind. This will help keep your energy levels up for the duration of the day, while also meaning you will be less likely to rush into giving incorrect answers due to being stressed.

Practise deep, abdominal breathing and relaxing your muscles (imagine you are breathing from your belly. This is how babies breathe and it is far more natural and conducive to a calm state of mind). Research mindfulness techniques to help you maintain a calm and collected mindset. There are great apps like *Calm* and *HeadSpace* that can help with this. If you start to tense up on the day, take a deep breath and try *telling* yourself to relax, this has been shown to lower stress levels and reduce physical tension.

No analysis paralysis

Analysing your own performance during the Assessment Centre can be very detrimental to your performance. If you are tempted to do this, promise yourself that you will not analyse how you think you are doing until *after* the day has finished. If you try to analyse how you think you are doing *during* the tasks, this will invariably take you out of the moment, impacting how you are performing on your current task.

Also, it will be a wasted effort that will only stress you. Since the tasks are still happening, it would be meaningless to try to take stock of how you think you have done, since it is still subject to change from moment to moment. It'll just stress you out without giving any useful conclusions as to how you have done.

Suspend any self-evaluation until you are on your way home afterwards. Especially do not discuss your performance with other candidates during the day, or let them discuss their performance with you. This would not only be unsettling, but just as unreliable, since other candidates also don't really know how they've done.

Let your enthusiasm shine

Being passionate is a key quality that recruiters and assessors look for in a candidate. They want people who are energised and excited to be there. This doesn't mean that you need to be hyperactive or frenetic, but do show that you are enthusiastic, and that you are excited by the opportunity to work there. You will need to know *why* the opportunity excites you, however, in order to be truly motivated to work there. Review your research into the employer and role. If you are not sure on this, revisit 2.2.2 Two Critical Steps and 2.2.5 Three Key Questions.

Excellence, not perfection

As a last word on mindset, **you don't need to be perfect** to succeed at an Assessment Centre. You *can* make mistakes. There is no such thing as the perfect candidate. This doesn't mean you shouldn't aim for excellence or try to minimise mistakes, but it does mean that you shouldn't start to worry or lose your composure if you do make a mistake.

Employers are simply looking for people with the right transferable skillset and personality fit that they can train up, through their grad scheme, to join their workforce. With that in mind, a successful Assessment Centre mindset is one where you are professional, calm and collected throughout the day, performing consistently throughout the tasks. Try to imagine that you have the job already, and that this is just another day.

In fact, that is exactly the scenario an Assessment Centre is trying to achieve - replicating a busy day as a graduate employee. So relax into the role, be professional in your answers, and focus on your own performance during the tasks.

Dress for success

The preparation for an Assessment Centre in terms of what to wear, and how you should act on the day, is exactly the same as for interviews. You should wear something professional and appropriate for the day, and your body language should be open, attentive and professional. Read Dress For Success from 2.6.1 Preparing for Interview for more on appropriate attire and body language.

Ask questions to make an impression (and find out useful information too)

Assessment Centres often include office tours and group lunches with some of the employer's personnel. These can be held by one or more of their graduate recruits from previous intakes, a member of their graduate recruitment team, or by someone senior.

Taking this opportunity to ask some questions about the employer and what it is like to work there, or what projects/clients they are currently working on, can be a great way to get useful information that might help you answer questions later on at interview. It is also a great way to demonstrate that you are keen to be there and interested in finding out more.

Although these parts of the day will not be formally assessed, showing interest might be noted and help you score brownie points, as well as helping you find out some useful information that might come into play at interview, if nothing else. As with anything, aim for a balanced approach, don't overdo it by asking too many questions. One or two would be a good number to aim for.

6.2 CASE STUDIES

What are case studies?

A case study presents a fictional scenario involving a problem question. You will be presented with several pieces of information outlining the case study. Contained within this extra information are clues and some red herrings as to what the solution should be. You are asked to identify a solution to the case study problem and justify your reasons for selecting it.

Case studies for graduate roles are predominantly non-technical and non-specialist; if you do need any technical awareness you will be told this by the recruiter beforehand. You should, however, be aware of the main issues for your industry and the employer you are applying to. The interviewer will expect you to know the broader issues at play in the industry; this is also a good way of scoring extra points by discussing the impact on stakeholders of some new piece of legislation or policy, or other topical market factors. It would also be a good idea to know all of the departments and major service offerings of the employer you are applying to, since some case study questions ask, "How can we use our services to help this client?". This should have been covered in your employer research, but refresh your knowledge, or cover it now, before you attend a case study task.

There is usually more than just one right answer to a case study task. This is because the exercise is mainly designed to see *how you think*. Are your answers rationally justified, is your thinking logical, have you considered the pros and cons of your position, and have you considered the pros and cons for the *alternative* positions as well? Other skills they will also look at are your ability to assimilate information quickly, your time management, and your communication skills when you come to present your response to the case study question.

Format of a case study exercise

A case study will present you with a scenario that has several potential answers. You will have a set period of time to read the case study materials and make notes. You are then given some time to prepare your answer, and finally you will present your answer. The presentation can take any of the following formats, depending on each employer's application process:

- Group discussion as part of the group interview;
- Written exercise; or
- A presentation or discussion at interview.

For some application processes you will have to complete a number of case study exercises. For example, you may have a case study set as part of a first interview, but then have to also complete a case study group exercise during an Assessment Centre.

Although each of these presentation *formats* have their own nuances, these can each be prepared for and tackled in their own way (see 2.5.6 Group Exercises, 2.5.4 Written Exercises and 2.5.3 Presentations). However, when it comes to the *case study itself*, the approach is always the same, and we will work through that here.

How to answer case study questions

Let's work through an example. You are given a case study and told that your employer has been instructed by one of their main clients to advise them; the client is looking to expand and acquire another company, there are three different options they are choosing from on which company to purchase.

Each of the three has their own advantages and disadvantages. Your task is to assess each option, and present an analysis and recommendation back to your client. So how do we go about answering this case study exercise?

Understand the question

Firstly, you should read the question through, slowly and thoroughly. Underline or highlight the key parts of it. Make sure you understand *exactly* what is being asked, before you start to form an answer. You would be surprised how many candidates rush in and start answering, wasting valuable time, before realising they've misunderstood the question. Or worse, not realising it at all. Nerves will play tricks on you during the pressurised environment of an Assessment Centre or interview. Take your time and be sure of what is being asked of you before you start to answer.

Read and highlight the case study materials

Once you've understood the task, read the case study material once through, carefully, from beginning to end. It will contain a wealth of information. In our example, you would be presented with details of three companies. Some of the information would be obvious and spelt out clearly, some of it would be more nuanced and only hinted at. As you read through a case study, identify what the key issues are, and who the stakeholders are. Stakeholders are any group of people who are impacted by the actions you propose to take (or not take). Impacted stakeholders may include employees, shareholders, customers, the general public, and local residents.

Building a framework for your answer (the Table Method)

Once you've understood the question and have read through the case study materials once, you should have an idea of what the main issues are and who the impacted stakeholders are. The next step is to start putting together a logically structured answer.

First, organise the information you have to make it easy for you to present your answer in a straightforward and clear way. The case study task is, after all, mostly an exercise to see how logical and organised your thinking is, and how you present your findings. If you organise your notes and analysis in a logical way, then your answer is likely to be logically structured as a result.

The Table Method we will now look at will organise all of the pertinent information along a logical framework. You won't present the table itself in your response, it is just a way to quickly dissect the information you need out of the text and organise it to structure your response.

Case study answers involve choosing one of the available solutions, and presenting your case for why you are recommending that particular option, and why you haven't selected the other possible solutions. We'll call each of these solutions 'options' in our table. In the first column we'll list the option you are presented with, this will represent each of the alternatives (option 1, option 2, option 3) you are given in your scenario.

In the second column we will list the 'Issues' in play: this includes things like policies and legislation, any redundancies that may result and any other implications you can think of resulting from that particular option.

For the third column, we'll list the impacted stakeholders. In the final two columns we'll capture strengths and weaknesses of each option as '+ves' and '-ves'. The table should look like this:

Option #	Issues	Impacted Stakeholders	+ves	-ves
Option 1				
Option 2				
Option 3				

You can now begin to populate each row of the table with the relevant information for each option. Once you've completed the table you can see, at a glance, all of the relevant information for each option. You can now begin to draft your answer.

Important note: keep an eye on the time while you are drawing up your table and populating it with the relevant information. Make sure you **leave yourself enough time** to complete your analysis and write up your answer in whatever format is required. It should take you less than 30 seconds to draw up the table. When you are populating it, you should only use key words like 'redundancies' or 'environmental impact', rather than writing out your notes in full. Remember that you won't be presenting the table, it is only a very good way to quickly capture all of the relevant information you need out of the case study, before you come to write your answer. This method is optional: if you have a different way of capturing and logically framing your answer that works better for you then use that instead.

Putting together your answer

The approach we'll look at now works for all kinds of case study presentations (written exercises, presentations and interview discussions), with the exception of the group interview. We discuss how to answer group interview questions and case studies in 2.5.6 Group Exercises

You should begin with a very short summary of the scenario, no more than a sentence or two. Don't waste valuable time by presenting back what the assessors already know. Something along the lines of "Our client, XYZ Corporation are considering between three different companies to purchase in order to expand their business. They have asked us to evaluate the available options and present back".

Now onto the main part of our answer. Work your way through each option, taking each one at a time. The best way to do this is to first outline the option, and then methodically discuss it by going over each of the columns in your table. You repeat this process three times (or for however many options you are given to consider). You should proceed along the following lines:

- Summarise the option **in brief** (showing the assessor you have understood it);

- Outline the issues that would arise from choosing that option;

- Identify the stakeholders affected and show how they are affected;

- Discuss the positives and negatives of picking this option;

- Give a conclusion: is this the option you are recommending overall, and why are you recommending or not recommending it? Make sure you definitely **do** make an overall recommendation by selecting one of the options. Although more than one option might look attractive in a case study, you should always make a definite decision one way or another and **pick one of the options.** Choose the one you think is the most reasonable, with the greatest amount of positives and the least amount of negatives, compared to the other options; and

- Repeat this process for each option until you have discussed through all of them.

Your final conclusion

You should already have made your recommendation as you proceeded through discussing each of the options. If you have done that then all that is left for you to do is reiterate your conclusion and say that you have selected it for the aforementioned reasons.

Some candidates opt to hold off from making a final conclusion until the very end of their case study presentation or write-up. This is not a good approach, since it disconnects the justifications you gave earlier on in favour of an option, from the conclusion you give at the end. Your assessor will have to cast their mind back (if it is a presentation) or leaf back through your answer (if it is a written exercise) to find the arguments you gave to justify your choice. This makes it seem like you've arbitrarily picked your solution rather than rationally justified your choice. You also run the risk of running out of time and not being able to make a final conclusion at all if you leave it until the end.

Once you have presented your answer back, you may be asked

some questions about your analysis. Remember that this is an exercise to see how you rationally justify your thinking. The table will come in useful in finding any information you need to answer questions. If you are unsure of a question, you can politely ask the assessor or interviewer to repeat it.

6.3 PRESENTATIONS

A presentation task is often included at Assessment Centre stage. It is usually between five and ten minutes, and can involve presenting to another group of candidates, an assessor or a senior member of staff. Some employers include a presentation task in the final interview. You will be told about the topic beforehand if this is the case.

Presentations can seem very daunting and stress-inducing, particularly if you don't like public speaking. You should plan how to use the time carefully. Common mistakes are to not prepare enough and run out of things to say, or to try to cram in all of your research and rush through your answer, trying to score as many points as possible as if it was a written exam.

Your communication skills are being tested here and your **delivery** is just as important as answering the content of the question. Let's look at some strategies that will help you score highly on presentation tasks.

- **Preparation:** the more you know your material in advance, the more confident you will feel giving the presentation. If you're given the topic a few days before the task, research it thoroughly: become an expert. If you're given some material to prepare on the same day as part of an Assessment Centre, go over all of it as much as you can in the time you're given. Learn the Table Method in 2.5.2 Case Studies and use it to rationally construct how you will structure your presentation.

- **Introduce yourself:** begin your presentation by introducing yourself and give a brief outline of what you will present. Even if you already know everyone in the room and have been talking with them all day, this is a good way to ease yourself into the presentation before you launch into the detail. It is also a good way to build a connection with your audience, which is our next point.

- **Connect with your audience:** make eye contact regularly, and with different people. Make a point of connecting with each person, don't rapidly shift your gaze from person to person, but don't stay too long with one person either. Be measured, and slow in your talking; do the same with the way you make eye contact. It will help each audience member feel like you are talking to them individually, and you will build a connection with them.

- **Take your time:** talk slowly. You may think you are speaking at normal speed, but your nerves are likely propelling you forward at breakneck velocity. Take your time: making fewer points in a confident, measured, and calm way is far better than rushing through and looking flustered.

- **Avoid fillers:** fillers are words we subconsciously use to buy time to think of what to say next. 'Um', 'err' and 'erm' are often used for this. Instead of a filler, take a short pause - this will give your brain the thinking time it needs, while also making you sound more calm and measured.

- **Dress for confidence:** wear something professional but also comfortable, something that will make you look the part, even if you don't necessarily feel the part. Dressing for success will help you feel like you fit in with the employer's organisation already and make you more confident on the day. See Dress For Success for more detail.

- **Occupy centre stage:** don't stand off to the side or awkwardly stand too far back from your audience. When you are presenting, step to the centre of the room and own it. Don't come across as too loud or aggressive, but be assertive, calm and confident.

- **Hold your ground:** some presenters have an awkward habit of constantly stepping backwards and forwards on the spot when they speak (I have seen this in countless presentations). It will distract the audience from what you are saying and make them focus on your movements instead. Hold your position, and if you feel the need to move around do it very sparingly. Avoid constantly pacing backwards and forwards as well; you can move every so often, but avoid constantly moving.

- **Body language:** presentation experts often recommend keeping your arms bent at 45 degrees with your hands neatly cradled together or holding a pen in front of you. This will help you to avoid fidgeting with your hands.

- **Relax:** take deep breaths and remember to relax. Use slow, abdominal breathing to relax you. Imagine you are breathing from your stomach. When you breathe in, imagine your belly is filling with air, relax your stomach muscles as your gut expands. When you breath out, slowly contract your stomach muscles so your gut pulls in. Do this slowly. If you watch babies, this is how they breathe. Shallow, chest breathing is how we have been conditioned to breathe as adults, and it is less relaxing. On each exhale, pause for four seconds before breathing back in; and on each inhale, pause for four seconds before breathing back out.

- **Don't evaluate yourself**: don't try to assess how your presentation is going while you're giving it. This is an easy way to trip yourself up and make mistakes. If you do make a mistake, you'll be busy evaluating its impact instead of focusing on giving a great presentation. Suspend self-judgement and critiquing while you are giving the presentation and evaluate it afterwards if you have to.

- **You don't need to be perfect:** if you make a mistake, don't dwell on it or analyse. Just calmly move on with the rest of your presentation.

- **Take water with you:** when you go up to give your presentation take a glass or bottle of water with you. You'll want this to hand in case the nerves start to dehydrate you. Taking a quick sip is also a good tactic to help you pause and gather your thoughts if you get stuck.

- **Be mindful of the time:** take a watch with you and put it on a table in front of you, or make sure you can see a clock in the room. Progress through your presentation in a slow, measured way without rushing. Structure your presentation beforehand to give you enough time to cover everything. If you have five minutes for example, then use 30 seconds for the introduction, 3 1/2 minutes for your main content, and 1 minute for your conclusion.

- **Invite questions at the end:** some interviewers will stop you to ask questions during the presentation. Don't let this fluster you: asking questions is usually a good sign the audience is listening to you and is interested in what you're saying. If your presentation is during a one-on-one interview, you want to make it more like a conversation than a presentation if possible anyway. At the end of your presentation, ask the audience if they have any questions. Make sure to do this after your presentation rather than during the short time you're given. Even if the recruiter intervenes to say your time is up, inviting questions will show you are prepared to answer them and are conscious of your audience.

Slide presentations

Some recruiters will invite you to create slides to support your presentation. If this is the case, keep your slides straightforward and simple. Try to use two to three slides, no more than five at a maximum. Include a handful of short bullet points on each slide rather than lots of text.

Make use of images or diagrams to break up the text and help with the visual appeal of the slide. Be careful to check that the image you include is either a diagram you have created your-self, or something that is not under copyright and is available in the public domain. If you include an image, make sure that it is professional and appropriate for the setting. Needless to say it should be relevant to your presentation and provide support to it.

If you are using slides in your presentation do not read from your slides. They are merely an aide for your presentation, they are *not* the presentation itself. Glance occasionally at your slides to help prompt you, but do not turn your back to the audience to read off the screen. Know what each point on your slide says and present it yourself: don't rely on your slides to convey the message.

The bullet points on your slide should only be very short talking points to help prompt you. They should never contain large chunks of text and all of the information you want to say. Instead, each bullet should just be enough to provide a teaser for the audience about what **you** will be saying. Bullets also have the duel function of structuring your presentation and reminding you what the next point you'll make will be.

This approach will keep the audience's attention on you during the presentation rather than on your slides. Remember, this is a presentation task, **not** a task in putting slides together. The assessors wants to hear **you** speak, rather than read the answer on your slides. Aim for simple, elegant and polished-looking slides.

Notes and supporting material

It is okay to take a few notes with you when you go up to give your presentation (unless your recruiter tells you otherwise). If you take your notes with you, glance at them very briefly and sparingly as you talk. Notes should only serve as an aide to your memory. Do not read directly from your notes, you will come off sounding monotonous.

Have your bullet-pointed presentation structure in front of you to remind you of each point you want to say. Do not take up anything you haven't written yourself, such as printouts of their graduate recruitment website.

Don't memorise

If you know your presentation topic beforehand, plan your presentation thoroughly, but avoid the temptation to fully write out your speech. If you try to memorise it, the nerves on the day will very likely trip you up and make you forget parts or freeze up entirely. Even if you printed out the whole thing to read from, you would sound very monotonous reading it off the paper. The assessors can spot this a mile off.

Instead, research your material thoroughly and try to become as expert as you can in your topic. This will help you feel confident presenting on it. Then put together a bullet-pointed structure for your presentation covering all the points you want to cover. Practise giving your presentation to friends or family over and over again, until you are calm and confident with your material and what you'll say.

6.4 WRITTEN EXERCISES

Written exercises are a good way for employers to gauge your communication skills, professionalism and problem solving. How you express yourself in writing will tell them a lot about you.

These types of exercise can take the form of writing an internal report, an e-mail to a senior colleague, a formal letter to a client or other party, or a simple list of bullet point findings in response to an internal e-mail request.

All of the following guidelines are relevant across each of these formats.If your written exercise involves a case study, be sure to review the information in 2.5.2 Case Studies as well as what we'll look at here.

Written exercise guidelines

One of the key things graduate employers are looking to assess is **your use of business writing**. As we saw during the application form stage, business writing does not mean using financial terms. It means being succinct, getting your points across in a concise and straightforward way. You should keep in mind the following points when drafting your written exercise answer:

- **Keep sentences short and to the point:** The longer the sentence, the more confusing it'll be. Business language is always short and to the point. Convey your message in the simplest way possible.

- **Use the active voice:** The active voice simply means starting a sentence with the *subject*. The subject is the person who is *doing* something in your sentence. It is the person who your sentence is about. For example, "Elizabeth went to the cinema" is in the active voice, since it starts with Elizabeth, who is the person doing the action in the sentence. If it were written "To the cinema went Elizabeth", apart from sounding like Jedi Master Yoda, it would be very confusing to read.

- **Avoid elaborate or academic language:** Essay writing is very different to writing a work e-mail. Academic writing is valued for its depth; however business writing is valued for its **brevity**, its ability to convey a message in a simple and straightforward way. Imagine you are employed at a major company and you are inundated daily with dozens of e-mails. You simply don't have the time to write elaborate or lengthy prose, and your recipients won't have the time to read it either. Keep your writing straightforward and simple.

- **Use a professional tone:** avoid trying to include humour or make the assessor laugh. Keep your content relevant at all times and the wording professional. Never use text speak.

- **Correct spelling, punctuation and grammar:** since this is an assessment, you will not be provided with a dictionary or spell checking facilities. Read through your work thoroughly and try to pick up on any mistakes before you submit it.

- **Structure your answers to follow a logical pattern:** usually written exercises ask you to make a recommendation out of several choices based on evidence you are given (see 2.5.2 Case Studies for how to do this). When you construct your answer, make sure that it flows coherently and logically. Stick to one overall topic per paragraph and work through each option one by one (instead of discussing them all at the same time).

Accessibility and extra time

If you are usually allowed extra time in exams then let the graduate recruiter know in advance of your assessment. You may need to bring along any relevant evidence to establish this on the day, or send it to them in advance. Employers are very accommodating and supportive in giving you the time you need to ensure a fair assessment.

Different openings and closings

How you begin and end your written exercise will depend on the format you are given.

Letters:

- If you **don't** know the name of the person you are writing to, use "Dear Sir/Madam" to open. Use "Yours faithfully" to close.

- If you **do** know the name of the person you are writing to, use "Dear Mr/Mrs/Miss/Ms X" to open (selecting the correct designation as appropriate). Use "Yours sincerely" to close.

- If this is a less formal letter (e.g. an internal company letter, and the person is known to you), you can use their first name e.g. "Dear Laura".

- Before starting your answer, you can preface it with, "Thank you for your letter dated...".

E-mail:

- If your task is to write an e-mail, it will usually be in response to an e-mail you have received. The usual scenario is to receive an e-mail from a manager or senior colleague asking you to make a recommendation. You can take your cue from the e-mail you receive as to the opening and closing:

- If the e-mail setting you the task begins with "Hi Lin", for example, and closes with "Kind regards, Charlie", you can open and close your e-mail in the same way. Similarly, if it opens with "Dear Miss Singh" and ends with "Yours sincerely, Mr. Stuart", then reply back in the same style.

- If you don't have a starter e-mail to take your cue from, err on the side of caution and go with the more formal "Dear" to open. As with letters, use "Sir/Madam" if you don't know their name. Use "yours sincerely" if their name is known or "yours faithfully" if unknown. You could also use "kind regards" to sign-off an e-mail.

It is nice to include a closing comment such as, "I hope this analysis is useful, please let me know your thoughts or if you have any changes or suggestions" if you are writing to a senior colleague. If you are writing to a client, use, "We look forward to hearing from you".

You should always include greetings and sign-offs, don't launch straight into your answer unless you have been asked to produce a report or list of notes only. Even if you are asked to produce a report, you may still need to include greetings and a sign-off depending how the task was set (e.g. in an e-mail or letter requesting the report).

Before you submit your written exercise, have a read through it again at least two or three times. Try to look at it from the recipient's perspective and see if what you have written is straightforward and reads the way you intended it to.

6.5 E-TRAYS

An e-tray is a simulated e-mail inbox exercise. It is designed to replicate a business scenario, and the subject matter is usually related to the industry of the employer giving the assessment. It is, in essence, a prioritisation task, designed to assess how effective your decision-making is under a time-pressured scenario. You will need to identify the issues that are the most critical and deal with them first as you make your way through the task.

Format of the e-tray

Nowadays, most e-tray exercises are in the form of a computerised assessment. Depending on the employer, however, you might still be presented with a paper-based 'in-tray' instead, though this is less common. The approach to how you should tackle each type is exactly the same.

In the task you will be presented with an e-mail inbox (this is your own inbox for the scenario, as if you are already an employee working there and receiving e-mails in the course of a regular working day). There will be a number of e-mails already in the inbox. Some of these have attachments, including reports, other e-mails, graphs and charts. Others will be marked for urgent attention. As the task progresses, new mails will come in.

Your task will be to work through the inbox and take the appropriate action required, as prompted in the e-mails. Typical actions include delegating to a colleague, forwarding to a more senior colleague, making a recommendation based on the information available to you, and providing an answer based on an attachment in another e-mail.

E-trays are usually multiple choice assessments: at the bottom of each e-mail you are given a selection of actions you can choose from. Select the action you think is the most appropriate and move onto the next mail. Since this is a time-pressured assessment, you may not have enough time to answer all of the e-mail actions, so you will need to prioritise and deal with the most urgent issues first and work your way downwards in order of priority from there.

As the task unfolds, a common scenario is to have a high-priority issue unfold requiring you to take action. It will be important to spot this and prioritise it as you move through the task.

Strategy and tips

- **Practise:** just like with psychometric testing, the amount of practise you do for an e-tray will have a direct impact on how you do on the day. Do practise e-tray assessments as much as you can until e-trays become second nature to you. Although the content and subject matter may be slightly different than the actual assessment you will sit, you can still refine your technique and get used to how an e-tray works.

- **Keep an eye on the time:** bearing in mind that this is a time-pressured assessment you will need to keep a very close eye on the time. Time management is a very easy thing to make a mistake on. Keep a close eye on the time as you work through the e-tray and pace yourself accordingly.

- **Open all attachments:** depending on the e-tray interface, you may be able to open all of the attachments and keep them open. Use drag and drop to move them to the side of the screen so they are easily accessible to you throughout the task. This will save you valuable time instead of hunting back through your inbox every time you need to refer to an attachment. Every second will count during the e-tray, so keeping your attachments open is a good strategy.

- **Deal with the priority mails first:** once you have

familiarised yourself with the scenario and any background e-mails you should read, see if you can spot the high-priority ones that are already in your inbox and deal with these first. They may be labelled as priority, or marked with a red exclamation mark next to the title in the inbox. Once the simulation gets underway, you will see new e-mails come in; keep an eye out for any marked as priority or urgent. You may end up with some red herrings though. Just because something is labelled 'urgent', it doesn't necessarily mean that it actually is. Sometimes the reverse is also true, with urgent e-mails coming through that are not actually marked as high priority. Exercise your judgement when prioritising, try to work out what the impact would be of not acting immediately. If you do spot urgent e-mails, tackle these first and come back to the others if you have time afterwards.

- **Use the elimination method for multiple choice:** similar to psychometric testing, if you are unsure which answer to select from the multiple choice options, eliminate the answers that you think are not correct one by one until you narrow it down to one answer.

E-tray practice tests

You can access free e-tray practice tests from the following:

- Assessment Day:
  http://www.assessmentday.co.uk/free/e-tray/index.html

- Job Test Prep: http://www.jobtestprep.co.uk/free-in-tray-exercise

6.6 GROUP EXERCISES

Group interviews look to test your team working, problem solving and communication skills. They are regularly included as part of Assessment Centres for law, accountancy and management consulting grad schemes. They are fast becoming the norm across all industries, however, so check your application process to see if a group exercise is part of yours.

The task set is usually built around a case study, occasionally it can be to construct something to solve a physical problem. Note that the case study type is much more common than the construction type task. Let's look at each type of group exercise in turn.

Case study group exercises

For this type of task, there is usually an overall brief, and then each candidate receives a separate and unique brief that only they will see. So, say for example there are ten candidates in your group exercise, you will be gathered around a table, and each of you will be given sheets of paper containing the case study brief and other information.

The overall case study brief will be the same for all candidates. There will be **another brief** containing information which is specific **only to you**; each other candidate will receive a slightly different brief.

As an example, let's say your group is asked to consider a location to build a new power plant (this is the overall brief). Each candidate's individual brief contains information about a different location (candidate brief). Some candidate briefs will contain what is obviously the wrong answer for the task.

Let's say you turn your brief over and look at it, and you are asked to present the case for selecting Town A as the location of the power plant. However, when you come to read the details you see that Town A already has a power plant, that the local population regularly protests about the negative impact on local wildlife and the environment, and that it is highly likely that planning permission to build a new plant would be strongly opposed. This is obviously not the solution to the overall task.

Some candidates mistakenly assume that the group exercise is calling for you to be as persuasive as possible; that you are being tested on your ability to convince the other candidates to take on your own individual brief at all costs; and that 'winning' this task will secure you victory in this stage of the application process. If you proceed along these lines, you will surely fail the task.

The fundamental thing the assessors are testing is to see how well you work in a *team*. They are looking for a team solution, and for you to be a contributive but influential part of the team. If you read your individual brief and it is clearly the wrong answer, when it comes your turn to speak in the task, briefly outline the facts for the rest of the group and then make your suggestion not to endorse this particular option and your reasons why. This is perfectly acceptable, and you will score highly for it, since they are also looking at how you reason and think, in just the same way as they are in a regular case study task.

A good response would be:

> "My brief was to investigate the possibility of building the plant at Town A. Town A has strong transport links across the south of England, meaning we can transport raw materials quite well, however the town already has a power plant. There is some evidence to show that there would be strong public opposition to the building of another plant, making it difficult for us to secure planning permission to build. If somehow we did manage to secure planning permission, there would still likely be a strong backlash from local residents, meaning that we might face reputational risk to our company in both the local, and possibly national, media".

In this way you have introduced your particular brief to the rest of your group, you have rationally weighed up the pros and cons, and then made a recommendation based on this. The assessors will have noted your calm demeanour and rational problem solving. This is what they are looking for. Being a team player does not mean having your way and securing your own agenda at all costs; it simply means doing what is best for the group.

If you do believe that your brief contains a viable solution to the problem, then recommend it, but be sure to point out the pros and cons that led you to make your decision.

When the other candidates are reading their briefs out and making recommendations, try to ask pertinent questions from time to time. The trick is to try to influence the group dynamic without being pushy or trying to dominate the discussion.

Construction type group exercises

For construction type exercises you will be presented with an array of materials to choose from such as sellotape, cardboard, Blu-tac and so on. This task is more around how you present your point of view, rather than whether or not you can actually solve the physical problem. An example would be that your group is asked to build a bridge to connect two tables within your interview room. The group is asked to design a practical and effective solution, and then to build it.

Owing to the adrenaline and pressure of the situation, some candidates will immediately want to rush off and start building things. If this is you, resist that urge until you have a firm design in place and a majority consensus from the group. If you are in a group and someone wants to rush off and start building, diplomatically rein them in and suggest you all come up with individual designs and then vote before starting to build anything.

Some candidates are more analytical and want to ensure you have the 'perfect' design. If left alone, they might end up spending most of the time trying to design a solution rather than actually building something. If you are this type of candidate, keep an eye on the time and make sure that you allow enough time to present your design to the rest of the team, and if they vote for yours, enough time to build it.

The construction type exercise opens up a little more opportunity for you to guide and influence the group than the case study type (although you can certainly do this in both tasks). As soon as the task starts, each individual candidate will want to follow their own instincts; some will rush off to pick up materials, others will keep to themselves and start drawing up designs, some will want to talk through the problem. Take advantage of this momentary confusion to suggest that everyone spends two minutes coming up with a design and then that you spend another couple of minutes voting on this as a group. This firmly establishes you as an influential team player.

Once you have all voted on the likely solution, see if you can volunteer yourself for a good team role like timekeeper or some other role. This, again, signals you out as a good team player. Remember that it doesn't matter if you actually succeed in solving the task and building your design (although not building anything at all might suggest something has gone wrong in your group's team working). Instead, the assessors want to see how well you perform in a team to communicate your point of view and diplomatically influence others to solve a problem.

Strategy and tips

- **Contribute in proportion to the group size:** the interviewers are looking for team players during this exercise. They don't want someone to dominate the group, nor do they want someone who doesn't contribute at all. Striking a balance is important. Resist the tendency to dominate the discussion in order to outperform the other candidates, this is a fast and sure way to take yourself out of contention and score negatively. As a rough guide, you should only talk in proportion to how many people are in the group. If there are ten candidates overall in your group exercise, then you should look to contribute 1/10th of the time. This doesn't mean you can't play an influential role, you can still influence the group and make yourself stand out, but it is the *quality* of what you say that matters, not the quantity.

- **Suggest each person take it in turns to present their view:** in the case study scenario, suggest that you all take it in turns to present your brief and recommendation, and then to vote for each one in turn (vote after each short presentation rather than at the end. The likelihood is the group will have forgotten all of the different options by the time you reach the end).

- **Don't get drawn in by difficult candidates:** it is quite likely that there will be at least one candidate who will try to dominate the proceedings. Resist the temptation to get drawn into heated discussions with that person, or trying to close them down. You are likely to enter into a game of trying to outdo each other. Instead, listen to what they have to say, be diplomatic and point out the merits of what they are saying, and why you might disagree, draw other people into the conversation who may be more quiet; suggest moving on to the next option due to the time constraints.

- **Invite others to contribute:** the sign of a great team player (and a good leader) is someone who brings out the best in the team. There may be some candidates who are being quiet, a good way to score points is to ask for their opinion and bring them into the discussion.

- **Speak early on:** say something within the first 30 seconds, or at least before a couple of minutes have elapsed at the very latest. Speaking early will break through the nerves and any fear you have on the day. The longer you leave it without saying anything, the easier it'll be for you to settle into a rhythm and remain too quiet for the rest of the task. The group exercise is about striking a balance between speaking and listening in proportion to the group size. Don't go too far the other way and not speak enough.

- **Be confident, clear and assertive, but don't dominate the discussion:** state your point of view in a straightforward, calm and confident manner. Imagine this is a business meeting and you already have the job. How would you behave then? How would you communicate with your colleagues? Always be calm and professional, listen to others, speak when you have to, never put anyone else or their opinion down. Contribute when you have something to say, and listen to what others are saying.

- **Be collaborative, not competitive:** a fundamental question the assessors will be asking themselves during this task is, "Can I work with this person, and can my team work well with this person?". There is a common misconception that the world of work, particularly in professional services, is cut-throat and competitive. This may have been true in the past, but thriving, successful businesses are those that foster a spirit of collaboration among their employees. Teams are more efficient that way, and employees are happier and more productive when they work in an encouraging supportive environment. Recruiters are looking for good team players; helping your team to succeed together will also help yourself to succeed.

- **Volunteer early for a team role:** try to volunteer early for a good team role, this is a fantastic way to show that you have great team-working skills. Suggest to the group at the start of the task that you act as timekeeper, since you all need to be very mindful of the time. Alternatively, see if there is a whiteboard or flip chart and pens in the room, and volunteer to draw up options on the board or paper. If you do manage to secure one of these roles, you will have to multi-task. Don't lose track of the time if you are the timekeeper, issue regular reminders at regular intervals (e.g. ten minutes to go, five minutes to go, one minute to go). The same is true if you are writing on the whiteboard of flipchart, listen to what the other candidates are saying while you are drawing things on the board. Be sure to contribute when you want to say something.

- **If all team roles are taken and things aren't going 'your way':** let's say you wanted to volunteer for timekeeper, or the person who will scribe on the whiteboard, but you have been beaten to the punch by other candidates in both cases. Let's also say that another one or two candidates seem to be dominating proceedings. Don't assume that it is all going badly for you or that it is too late to score well in the task. You can still help the team to work together and make decisions without **any** of these roles. Make suggestions, draw others into the conversation, ask the timekeeper how much time is left. Keep working towards a group victory. This task is as much about not losing the task as it is about winning it. All you have to do is be a contributive member of the team, someone who helps the group solve the overall problem in a productive, collaborative way, rather than someone who dominates the proceedings.

7 INTERVIEWS

Being invited for interview is a great sign that the employer likes what they see in you so far. It is an opportunity for the employer to verify for themselves what you've put on your application form, and to try to get a sense of you as a person.

At Assessment Centres, they look to test specific skills, like team working, time management, organisation and communication skills. But at interviews, not only will they look to revisit your application form answers, but they will try to get a sense of you as a person, including your motivation, how passionate you are about getting the role, your professionalism and whether you would be a good personality fit for the organisation.

Types of interview

There are a variety of different types of interview commonly given to graduates:

- Telephone and Video Interviews;
- Competency-Based Interview;
- Strengths-Based Interview;
- Case Study Interview; and
- Final or Partner Interview.

The type of interview you are given will depend on what stage you are at in the application process. This will also depend on the employer you have applied to, since each employer's recruitment process is slightly different.

The first four types of interview in our list tend to occur as a first stage interview. This can either be a preliminary step before being invited to Assessment Centre, or part of the Assessment Centre itself. If a final or partner interview is part of the process, it will always be the last step in being considered for an offer.

In the pages that follow, we will work through how you can prepare for each of these types of interview, and what you can do to score highly in them. But before that, let's look at some general things you can do to help you succeed at interview stage.

7.1 PREPARING FOR INTERVIEW

As we saw earlier in this book, preparation is absolutely fundamental to succeeding in any graduate employer's application process. Nowhere is this more true than at interview stage. This applies equally to first stage interviews and final interviews. Let's look at some of the things you can do to help you prepare:

Revisit and refresh your research

Re-read 3.2 Two Critical Steps and 3.5 Three Key Questions. As we saw in Part 1, you should be highly knowledgeable about: **the employer, their grad scheme, the role you are applying for, and their competencies.** You should use this knowledge to prepare your answers for the Three Key Questions: **'Why you?'**, **'Why us?'** and **'Why this role?'**. Giving your answers to these questions should be second nature to you by the time you come to interview.

You'll need to make your answers specific and personal to *you*. Answering any one of these questions with just what is written on their website or promotional materials will not be good enough with any decent interviewer. Instead, you'll need to use that content, but make it specific to you. Why are *you* excited about this employer and this role, and why should they specifically hire *you*.

For example, don't just say, "the upcoming work you'll be doing with Apple is really exciting to me". You need to say *why*. If you are applying for a technology role, you can say something like, "I am excited about the prospect of working with your diverse client base, including clients like Apple, since this will allow me to work at the forefront of the technology sector. My time as part of my university's computing society enabled me to hone my skills in...etc.".

As part of the 'Why us?' question, refresh all of your research on the company itself. See who their main clients or products are. Have a look in the news to see if there is any new activity regarding them in the press. (search Google News for the employer's name and see what comes up). If you spot anything positive that looks interesting, you could mention it in the interview. Steer clear of anything that is negative. Every employer will have negative press from time to time; it is better not to discuss this unless your interviewer brings it up.

If you spot an interesting-looking positive story, however, about a new deal, product or service they are involved in, then you can mention it as a part of your motivation for applying. It will show you're keen on this specific organisation and that you have done your research. If it is a relatively recent news article your interviewer may not have heard about it themselves yet. Be prepared to go into detail on anything you mention at interview as they may ask you to elaborate, so research thoroughly.

Know the employer's competencies

Revisit 3.3 Competency-Based Applications and read 7.2.1 Competency-Based Interview. Know the competencies like the back of your hand. Have at least two STAR-type stories to hand (one positive and one negative/constructive) for each. Even if you don't have a competency-based interview, you will likely have to answer questions about how your experiences match the skills the employer is looking for. This is exactly what competencies are, even if they are called something different or not referred to as 'competencies' in the interview.

Your application form and/or CV

Good interviewers and recruiters will know your application form or CV thoroughly. They may even have it printed out and in front of them during the interview. Make sure you know exactly what you've written there. Print out a copy and go over it; try to spot things they may ask you questions on.

7.1.1 DRESS FOR SUCCESS

Making a good first impression is important in helping you establish a rapport with your interviewer. A large part of this is your appearance. This says a lot about you, and it is dependent on what you wear.

Check with the graduate recruitment department of the employer to find out what dress code is expected for the interview. In general, erring on the side of caution and wearing something more conservative and business formal is advisable for interviews, even for industries known to prefer less formal office wear (unless you are specifically told otherwise by the employer's graduate recruitment team). Don't leave choosing your outfit until the last minute, have your clothes picked out several days in advance.

For Women	For Men
A business suitable dress or trouser suit should be worn. Always wear tights with a skirt, even in summer, and aim for a conservative length if you do wear a skirt. Hair and nails should be neat and tidy. Any jewellery should be minimal and conservative. Cover any tattoos. Wear comfortable shoes, avoid heels that are too high. Some make-up is okay but keep it minimal.	Wear a black or dark navy suit with a tie. Your tie shouldn't be too colourful. It is okay to have a tie with a pattern on it, but something striped or checked, avoid anything with characters, logos or images. Try to be clean shaven if possible, and have short or tidy hair. If you have any tattoos make sure they are covered. Wear dark, conservative socks and polished work shoes.

You don't need to rush off and buy designer clothing, but aim to look professional and business-like in what you wear. Try to look as if you are *already* employed there. Choose an outfit that both looks good and is *comfortable* for you to wear; this combination will help increase your confidence on the day. Avoid anything loud, colourful, revealing, or unprofessional.

7.1.2 BODY LANGUAGE

During an interview, your body language can either contribute or detract in a large way from what you are saying. If you say, "I'm really excited about the opportunity to work here in the future", but your arms are crossed, you are looking down and not making eye contact with your interviewer while you say it, that doesn't convey passion or enthusiasm to your interviewer.

If, on the other hand, you're leaning slightly forward, are smiling and making eye contact, this shows you are animated and really are excited about the opportunity to work there. Your body language should always be in accordance with what you are saying, and in an interview context everything you say should be positive. Never say anything negative, particularly about any other people or employers, this will come across as unprofessional.

Use an open and relaxed posture. This suggests that you are in a friendly and open state of mind, ready to be asked questions and volunteer answers. It also shows you are acting calmly under pressure. Being relaxed doesn't mean you are too open; guys, please avoid 'man-spreading' by spreading your legs too wide apart.

Never slouch in your seat or fold your arms behind your head. But do keep an open posture, meaning don't fold your arms (which conveys defensiveness). Either have one hand folded on top of another, or one hand on the table in front of you and the other on your lap. A good trick is to loosely hold both ends of a pen with your hands. This will stop you from fidgeting or interlocking your fingers.

Try to lean forward slightly and have a relaxed smile. If you find yourself tensing up, take a deep breath from your belly and try to relax your muscles.

Use active listening. When your interviewer makes a point, smile and nod. Have good eye contact, but again aim for equilibrium with it, don't stare too intently or for too long, but also avoid having too little or no eye contact. You want a balance and equilibrium in all that you do.

The handshake

When you greet your interviewer, you should smile, introduce yourself and shake hands. There are two extremes you should avoid when it comes to shaking hands. The first is the 'hand-crusher'. Aim for a firm handshake. Some people have interpreted 'firm' to mean that you should squeeze your interviewer's hand as tightly as you can until their eyes water. They will not be impressed by this. Firm, in this context, means not too strong and not too light.

The opposite extreme is the 'sloppy' handshake. There is nothing worse when it comes to shaking hands than a sloppy handshake, one that's really loose or just involves missing and awkwardly grasping someone's fingers. Aim for a palm-to-palm handshake, applying *some* pressure, not too much and not too little.

How you shake hands will convey something of your personality to the interviewer (regardless of whether it is true or not, they will still think along these lines). Too firm a handshake and you'll come across as aggressive, possibly even adversarial. Too weak a handshake may convey evasiveness or insecurity. If you have any doubts, try to practise a few times on a friend or family member before your interview.

7.1.3 MINDSET

Interviews can be nerve-wracking experiences. As we saw with Assessment Centres, interviews can seem like an exam where everything is on the line. If you blow it, then your application journey is over, at least for this particular employer. It's tempting to think that each of your answers to interview questions should be perfect to succeed. Let's look at how you can develop a more balanced mindset conducive for interview success.

No such thing as a perfect first date

Thinking you need to be perfect is the wrong attitude to take if you want to succeed at interview. Avoid thinking that you can't make mistakes during the interview, or that every answer needs to be perfect. Instead, approach each interview like it's a 'getting to know you' conversation with your interviewer. That's all it is, you're getting to know the employer to see if you want to work for them, and they're getting to know you to see if they want to work with you.

It's a bit like a first date. If you approach a date like an exam, then you'll be very nervous and tense. The likelihood, is that neither you nor your date will have a good time. But if you look at it like you're just getting to know someone, then the pressure is off. The world isn't at stake; if you aren't suited to each other then you're better off knowing that sooner rather than later. If you think you need to be perfect, you'll try to be something you're not (because none of us are perfect), and this will inevitably lead to problems further down the line if a relation-ship develops.

The exact same thing is true of an employer-employee relation-ship. If you try to be perfect during the interview, you'll only stress yourself out and vastly reduce your chances of succeed-ing. If by some rare chance you manage to succeed with this strategy and receive an offer, you might still be doing yourself a disservice in the long run. All of this will be a wasted effort if you find yourself in a job you aren't suited to, or at an employer you don't want to work for.

The best way to find these things out early is to get a sense for the employer during the application process, and especially at interview; that way you will be able to make an informed choice about whether you should accept an offer at this employer when you come to receive one.

It's okay *not* to know something!

Believe it or not, it's actually okay not to know the answer to an interview question (provided this is the exception rather than the rule). If your interviewer asks you something you don't know the answer to, then always answer truthfully by saying you don't know.

The interviewer will know if you try to make something up, or awkwardly muddle through an answer. Just be honest and say something like, "I'm sorry but I don't know the answer to that, but I can tell you what I would do to find out". Your interviewer will value your honesty. They may even have asked you a question they know you can't answer to see how you respond.

When you're working at a graduate employer, both as part of your grad scheme and beyond, you will face things every day that you won't know the answer to. In the course of your employment you will constantly be learning on the job. So it's fine not to know the answer to something at your interview.

This doesn't mean that you should not prepare or thoroughly do your research. It does mean, however, that if you get asked a question on something that you just don't know, it's fine to take this approach.

Some interviewers have even been known to *teach* candidates during interview; and these were successful candidates who received offers later on. Remember, in an ideal situation, you're aiming for a *collaborative conversation*, back and forth, rather than a polarised question and answer format. However, even if you don't get a back and forth conversation, don't let this discourage you. Some interviewers prefer a more formal style; this doesn't mean you aren't building a rapport with your interviewer.

Look for the positives in every experience

Never say anything negative in an interview. Always be positive and optimistic; employers are looking to hire positive and optimistic people, since they are more personable, making them easier to work with. If you have had a setback in the past which the interviewer asks you about, talk about what you learnt from it, how it motivated you or set you on a more productive path. Every setback can be seen positively from a different point of view.

Ask questions

It's good practice to ask questions, either during the interview if suitable, or afterwards. It will show the employer that you are eager to find out more about them and really are passionate about working there. It is also good to ask the interviewer about their own specific experiences and expertise. Not only will it flatter them (who doesn't like to talk about themselves to some extent?), but again it will show your passion for the work.

7.2 TYPES OF INTERVIEW

7.2.1 COMPETENCY-BASED INTERVIEW

We discussed earlier on in Part 2 how competency-based interviews are the most common interview for graduate roles. We also saw that competencies are transferable skills valued by graduate employers. You can gain these skills in a number of ways, from academia to extra-curricular interests and hobbies. Common examples of competencies include **team work, time management, communication and presentation skills**. In this section, we will look specifically at how to prepare for, and pass, a competency-based interview.

Note:

Recruiters will not say to you, "Can you show me how you've used the 'competency' of team-working". 'Competency' is a word used by the recruitment industry, but rarely used with candidates directly. Instead, they will ask something like, "Can you give me an example of a time where you have worked effectively within a team to achieve a goal?". They can also switch a competency to the negative and say, "Can you give me an example of a time when you worked in a team and things didn't go so well?".

Identifying an employer's competencies

If you haven't already done so, your first step in preparing for a competency-based interview is to identify the employer's competencies. These are usually listed on the graduate recruitment section of their website, although they won't refer to them directly using the word 'competency'. You'll find them under sections titled 'What we're looking for', you can also spot them based on role descriptions such as 'A day in the life of a trainee/analyst/graduate joiner'. Look out for things like communication, networking and ability to handle competing deadlines. These will be competencies. Make a list of each one you come across, keeping this list separate for each employer. Although they will be very similar, each employer's list of competencies may not overlap in all cases, and some may have employer-specific ones.

Preparing your response

Once you've identified the employer's competencies, you now need to show, via examples from your own life, how you have those competencies, and also how you have used them. The best way to prepare is to create a table matching up the employer's competencies with relevant examples from your own experience.

You should try to identify at least two examples of each competency, in case they ask you for more than one example. Try to avoid drawing too heavily on the same example repeatedly.

Competency	Examples of demonstrating the competency
Team Working	• Playing on a local basketball team. • Having a role organising and running your university's drama society.
Commercial Awareness	• Being university treasurer for the university film society. • Working on a till at a shop, being aware of the financial incomings and outgoings of a business.
Problem Solving	• Developing ideas for fund raising for a mental health charity. • Working out how to improve response times working at your part time job handling customer queries by telephone.
Communication and Presentation Skills	• Having a volunteer job as a museum tour guide. • Teaching gymnastics to children.

The examples listed in the table are varied. This is to illustrate that you can draw on experiences from a range of different areas, including university societies, sports, hobbies, part-time jobs, travel experiences and so on.

The more varied and diverse examples you bring, the better. This is because it will differentiate you from other candidates.

Everyone applying for the same role will already have the academic entry requirements needed, so using academic examples will not make you stand out. Graduate employers want rounded candidates who have multiple and diverse interests. This is because firstly, it makes for a more interesting colleague to work with. And secondly, employers know that healthy interests outside of work make for a better work-life balance, giving you better coping mechanisms to deal with the natural stresses that occur in every line of work.

That being said, it is okay to use academic examples if you have any particularly interesting ones that other candidates are unlikely to have, or if you are really struggling to evidence a particular competency from non-academic activities (you might not have had chance to give a presentation in a setting outside of academia, for example).

You should now have a table listing the employer's competencies and around two examples of how you have evidenced using those competency skills. Next we will look at a few examples of competency interview questions, before moving on to look at the methodology needed to answer them.

Competency interview questions

You will never be asked at a competency interview to simply 'list examples' of how you have met a competency. Instead, you will be asked to describe a time where you have used that competency. Remember that interviewers and recruiters will not refer to the skills they look for as 'competencies' when they talk to you. But, they will still be assessing you on the basis of competencies. Typical examples of these types of question are:

- Tell me about a time when you worked in a team to achieve a common goal;

- Tell me about a time when you used your communication skills to deliver a difficult message;

- Can you think of an example where you were faced with multiple deadlines and pressures? Tell me about the outcome;

- What was a time when you had to work with difficult personalities? How did you handle the situation and what was the outcome?

The interviewer can also ask competency questions in the negative. They can do this for any competency:

- Tell me about a time where you had to work in a team to achieve a common goal, but you were unsuccessful. What went wrong and what did you learn from the experience?

The STAR Method

Interviewers for competency-based interviews will not be looking for you to list a litany of examples where you feel you have demonstrated having a particular competency skill. Instead, they want you to stick to just one example, and elaborate on it; set the scene, tell them what the task at hand was, and what you individually did to achieve a positive result. This will tell them far more about you than if you simply list off a stream of examples. There is a specific methodology for doing this, and it is called the STAR method.

STAR is an acronym; it stands for:

- **Situation:** set the context, what was the setting and who was involved?

- **Task:** what was the challenge you faced?

- **Action:** what action did you take to overcome that challenge. Note that it is action *you* took, not your team. It's super important that you are the hero of this story, it is you who is being interviewed, not your team.

- **Result:** what was the outcome at the end?

What the above does is *tell a story*. And that's exactly what recruiters want to hear. Stories provide meaning; they are compelling. We identify with the heroes in the stories we read, watch and listen to. By structuring your answer in this way you take the recruiter on the same journey you went through in over-coming the particular challenge in the first place.

Rather than just saying, "I successfully helped raise funds for my local mental health charity", you should take them on the journey of how you went about doing that, the challenges you faced, the setbacks and difficult personalities involved, the actions you took, the way you went about doing things, and ultimately the triumph you felt at the end having successfully achieved your goal.

Notice the emphasis is on what *you* did. Even if it is a question about teamwork, you need to talk about what *your* role was within the team (after all, you are the one being interviewed, not your team). Make sure your role in the examples you give was substantial and contributive enough, even pivotal, to the end result. Let's look at an example:

Recruiter: Can you tell me about a time when you worked in a team to achieve a goal?

Candidate: As part of my university taekwondo society, I wanted to help raise money for us to go to the European championships (**Si**tuation). We were about £500 short of our goal (**T**ask). I had the idea that we could hold a taekwondo demonstration in the local community and ask for donations. The team liked the idea. I then planned how the event would go and organised all of the logistics(**A**ction). My team members and I then worked together to choreograph a demo and put the plan into action. The high street demo was really successful, we managed to raise just over £570 (**R**esult). We were able to make it to the European championships and won three gold medals in the sparring, and I won one of them!

Answering negative questions using the STAR method

Your interviewer asks, "Give me an example of a time when you worked in a team and things **didn't go so well**". This is a difficult question to answer, since you run the risk of making yourself look bad. The trick to this type of question is to **always end your response with a positive outcome**, even though you are being asked to discuss a negative one. You should also always avoid being negative about anyone else (this is a fundamental part of acting professionally).

Interviewers ask questions in the negative like this to see how you deal with adversity, difficult circumstances and difficult people. They also want to check how responsible you are, whether you blame things on others when things don't go so well, or whether you take ownership and learn from your mistakes.

Let's look at the question again. The interviewer is asking for an example of a time 'when you worked in a team and things didn't go so well'. The second part of the STAR method asks you to identify a task. In order to answer negative-type interview questions all you need to do is elaborate on the task step a little more by discussing some of the challenges you faced in greater detail. Once you have done that, you will have addressed the 'negative' requirement of the question. You can then go on to talk about how you learnt from this, took action, and turned things around to ultimately achieve a positive result.

In this way, you will have answered the negative-type question, while still ending on a positive outcome. It also demonstrates your capability to evaluate a situation, learn from it in the moment, and then put what you have learnt into practice to achieve a positive outcome. Let's use the example from earlier to see how we can elaborate on the task section and answer the negative-type question. The new parts are in **bold**:

> **Interviewer:** Give me an example of a time when you worked in a team and things didn't go so well.
>
> **Candidate:** As part of my university taekwondo society, I wanted to help raise money for us to go to the European championships (situation). We were about £500 short of our goal (task). **It was a difficult time for the team as there weren't any good ideas and there was disagreement about how we should go about raising the funds we needed. Some of the team members were even talking about leaving and joining a different team.** I had the idea that we could hold a demonstration in the local high street and ask for donations, the team liked the idea. I then planned how the event would go and organised all of the logistics (action). I used my communication skills to persuade my other team members that this was a good idea and it could work. I also delegated the tasks in a way that made us all work together to achieve the common goal. **I learnt a lot about team working from this experience and how to carefully manage**

different challenges and personalities when things don't go well to achieve a common goal in the end. The high street demo was really successful, we managed to raise just over £570. As a result we were able to make it to the European championships, we won three gold medals in the sparring and I won one of them!

This answer ticks the box of giving an example of a time when 'things didn't go so well'. By elaborating more on the challenges faced during the task section, the negative aspect is addressed. Learning from challenges and applying this feedback is key in these types of questions. In the answer, the applicant states that they learnt from the experience through improving their teamwork skills.

Notice how a couple of other competencies are also smuggled into the answer, such as communication and delegation skills. It's good to include other competencies in your answers where relevant, providing it is not overdone.

7.2.2 STRENGTHS-BASED INTERVIEW

Although less common than the competency-based interview, strengths-based interviews are gaining in popularity with graduate employers. These types of interview are focused on getting to know you as a person, what your interests are, and what motivates you.

Recruiters have recognised that candidates are increasingly aware of the competency-based approach and are preparing well-rehearsed, STAR-type answers. The strengths based interview still looks to try to identify your skills, but it seeks to do so by finding out about your interests and passions, rather than directly asking you about the skills you believe you've gained from them.

Even though this is different to a competency-based interview, the interviewer is still trying to find out about:

1. The type of skills you have; and
2. Whether you are a good personality fit for their organisation.

Typical strengths-based questions include:

- What types of activities motivate you?

- What do you like doing in your free time?

- What types of activity are you good at?

- What types of things tend to get left on your to-do list and not finished?

- What were your favourite subjects at school?

- Tell me about an accomplishment you are particularly proud of; and

- What would count as a successful day for you?

There are no right or wrong answers to this type of question. Your interests contribute to making you unique, they motivate and drive you. Be sure to answer with *genuine* interests. Don't avoid talking about things you're really interested in just because you think the employer values some interests over others, or you think your hobby or interest is somehow less valid.

Trying to feign interest in something you're not passionate about is a good way to fail the interview. Your interviewer can tell whether you are genuinely passionate about something or not. They are trying to hire people who would bring that same passion to the job.

Preparing for a strengths-based interview

- In the same way as preparing for a competency-based interview, draw up a table or list of all of your accomplishments, hobbies and interests. Include academic, sports and other extra-curricular clubs and hobbies in your list.

- Identify what competencies the employer is looking for. Although this is not a competency-based interview, the interviewer is still trying to find out whether you would be a good fit for their organisation.

- Try to match up your hobbies to particular skills the employer is looking for, e.g. team working, communication skills, time management, people skills, and so on. Don't try to prepare STAR-type answers as you would for a competency interview, just have your

hobbies matched up so if you are asked to elaborate on
the strengths your interests give you, you will have
them in the front of your mind.

- During the interview, let the conversation unfold
  naturally. Think of it less like an interview and more
  like getting to know someone. The interviewer is trying
  to get a sense of your personality. The best way to let
  your personality come across is just to let the interview
  unfold like a conversation.

- Let your passion shine through. When you are asked
  about your interests, show your natural enthusiasm for
  them, tell your interviewer what excites you about
  them. Ultimately, the interviewer wants to get a sense
  of whether you'd fit in with their organisation. Them
  feeling a good sense of rapport with you, and
  understanding you as person, will largely inform their
  opinion of you. The interviewer will be able to better
  relate to you if they have a sense of your interests and
  why you like those interests. This also helps them
  identify what drives you, and whether it would be the
  same sorts of things that this job offers.

- Let the interviewer draw the connections between your
  hobbies and the skills they give you. If you are asked to
  spell them out directly, or you think it will help you to
  identify them directly, then do so.

7.2.3 TELEPHONE AND VIDEO INTERVIEWS

After successfully completing the application form and psychometric testing, some graduate employers will invite you for a telephone or video interview. This is usually with a member of their graduate recruitment team rather than a member of their business; however business personnel have been known to conduct telephone interviews, depending on the employer. It is okay to ask your graduate recruiter who the interview will be with in advance of the interview.

The purpose behind a telephone or video interview is to assess your communication skills. Recruiters will look to see whether you can get your points across clearly, concisely and in a professional way. The call will usually last around 15 minutes.

Although telephone interviews can be quite straightforward, make sure you prepare thoroughly and as completely as possible: you don't want to fail in your application by letting yourself down here.

How to pass a telephone/video interview

These are the key steps you should take to give yourself the best chances of success:

- **Prepare the Three Key Questions:** if you've prepared enough, then you should score top marks when you are asked any one of these. Ensure that your passion for their organisation and this particular role comes through in your voice. Sometimes a person can say one thing but their voice and energy levels suggest they think the opposite. Make sure you sound enthusiastic. If this is a video interview, be sure to look engaged and interested. Smiling as you speak can make you sound a lot more confident when you talk (even if you are feeling nervous). A good night's sleep before the interview can make a huge difference as well.

- **Research:** go over your research thoroughly. Know what is unique about this employer and why you have applied to them.

- **Your competency table:** as we saw in 3.3 Competency-Based Applications and 7.2.1 Competency-Based Interview, make sure you know your table matching your experiences to this employer's competencies. Even if this is not strictly a competency-based interview, competencies are still a primary method for assessing graduates, so it is always a good idea to be prepared in case you get asked a competency-based question. Check that you have covered and included examples and STAR method stories for all of the competencies they look for, and all of the wider industry competencies. Include a few extra ones for good measure: it never hurts to be extra prepared in case they ask you to evidence a competency not explicitly listed on their graduate website.

- **Logistics:** before you have the call, make sure that you are somewhere quiet and will not be disturbed. Tell your family or flatmates that you are having an interview and that you are under exam conditions during this time period. Ask them politely if they could limit any noise during that time. Check before the call that you have good phone reception and that you have charged up your phone battery. Try to use a headset rather than holding a phone to your ears. If you use a headset, test it out on another call beforehand to check the sound comes through clearly. If this is a video interview, check that your camera and any other equipment works correctly beforehand.

- **Dress the part:** although in a telephone interview your interviewer will not be able to see you, dressing for work makes a big difference to a speaker psychologically. It will make a difference to how you sound. If you dress in business clothing, you will likely sound more polished and professional than if you were in casual wear. Needless to say, if you are having a video interview, you will need to dress the part, in exactly the same way you would if you were having an in-person interview.

- **Take your time:** speak clearly and confidently, and don't rush your answers. Remember they are looking to test your communication skills. Being calm and composed while you deliver a message is a valuable trait that businesses look to recruit, and that is what they are testing during a telephone interview. If you don't hear a question very well then it is okay to ask the interviewer politely to repeat it; this might also give you some valuable seconds to think if they've asked you a question you don't know the answer to immediately.

- **Stay calm:** if you are asked something you don't know the answer to, stay calm and don't panic. If it is a competency you haven't prepared for, look through your list of competency examples and see if you can adapt one of those responses to meet the new question. For example, you're asked to tell them about a time when you had to use your negotiation skills to solve a problem and you haven't prepared for this competency. Look back over your competency table and you'll likely be able to adapt another communication-based or teamwork example to demonstrate this competency. If you are asked something that's not competency-based and you don't know the answer, then say you don't know but tell the interviewer how you would go about finding out. They are looking for honesty and integrity rather than candidates trying to muddle their way through an answer they don't know.

- **Ask questions:** asking questions is a very useful tactic for any interview. Asking questions shows that you are interested in the company you are applying for and the work they do. If you have a telephone interview with a graduate recruiter rather than a member of the business, it isn't really applicable to ask them questions about their work in the business, since their knowledge and work revolves around recruitment. You can, however, ask them lots of questions about the grad scheme, like what the training involves, whether you get a chance to travel as part of the induction and so on.

7.2.4 FINAL INTERVIEW

The final or partner interview is the last remaining step in your application process. There are no more assessments after this, and all that remains is waiting to hear back on whether you have been successful in your application. Depending on different employers' recruitment processes, final interviews are sometimes given on the same day as the Assessment Centre, but they can also be held at a future date.

The interview will always be with a senior person in the business. The term 'business' here means someone who actually works in the role or department you are applying for. Any of your earlier interviews in the process might have been given by someone who works in HR or the graduate recruitment team. But the final interview will be with a senior manager, director or partner who actively works day-to-day in the field you are applying for.

The interview might involve a task, like giving a briefing or presentation. But it could also be an ordinary interview, with no special task. If a task is involved, you will be told about this beforehand. Be sure to check with the recruitment team or HR in advance what the format for the interview will be if you are unsure. If you have to give a presentation or discuss a case study, the topic or materials are usually given to you a couple of days beforehand.

Preparing for your final interview

The best way to approach a final interview is to look at it like a synoptic exam. Synoptic comes from the word 'synopsis', meaning that any earlier stage might be covered in this assessment, making it a kind of summary. You should be prepared for the interviewer to ask you questions about any part of the application process, including the application form, covering letter or CV you submitted right at the very beginning. They might also test some earlier part of the application process, such as by asking a competence-based question.

They will not, however, test you on any of the psychometric assessments or ask you to repeat an e-tray. Even if there is a set task or format for the final interview, like giving a presentation, be prepared for the interviewer to go off-script and ask you about any earlier part of the process.

Let's look at how you can prepare:

- **Review your application:** make sure you know your application form inside and out. Have it printed out and review every part of the answers you gave, including your academic history and personal details. If you included a CV or covering letter, review these as well. Be prepared to answer questions on these.

- **Review your knowledge on the employer:** since your final interview will be given by someone senior, they will be highly bought into the strategy, vision and culture of this organisation. They may have worked there for several years. Be prepared for them to test your understanding of the organisation, including its key service offerings and products, place in the market, unique selling points and key differentiators. You don't need to be an expert, but you need to show the interviewer that you've done your research, know what makes this place unique, and are keen to work there. Have a look at the employer's graduate website and their main site. The information there should be more than enough to give you a good understanding of the organisation.

- **Review your knowledge of the role:** have a thorough and in-depth understanding of the requirements of the role you are applying for. You should know what type of tasks you would be expected to do in the course of the role. Knowing what a typical day would look like would also be useful. The graduate recruitment website (or graduate recruitment section of the main website) for this employer will have information on the role requirements. You can also look at competitor employer websites for the same role since the types of tasks will largely be the same providing it is for the same or a very similar role, in the same field of work and industry.

- **Review your knowledge of the grad scheme:** the interviewer will want to see that you are keen to be offered a graduate role there. This includes not only showing you are enthused by the wider organisation and the specific role you have applied for, but also their grad scheme. Knowing what the benefits of the organisation's grad scheme are, and specifically why they matter to you, are important in answering any questions on this. Talking about the training opportunities available, the variety in the scheme and opportunities for varied and challenging work at the same time is a good example of how to answer any questions on why you find their grad scheme attractive.

You'll notice that the points we've just looked at mirror the **Three Key Questions** we looked at earlier. This is not a coincidence. You can expect these questions to come up, sometimes in various different ways throughout your final interview.

Remember that they are:

1. **Why should we hire you? (Why you?)**
2. **Why do you want to work at this organisation? (Why us?)**
3. **What attracts you to this role? (Why this role?)**

These questions are fundamental. No employer will hire you if you can't answer these questions. The 'Why you?' question, tells them what you have got to offer. Your answer to the 'Why us?' question shows them that you are keen to work there, since they only want to hire people who are passionate about joining their organisation. And thirdly, 'Why this role?', will show the interviewer that you are aware of, and familiar with, the day-to-day realities and expectations of the job, that you won't balk and quit right away after they have gone to the trouble of hiring you because you didn't know what to expect.

Being thoroughly prepared along the lines of these three questions is absolutely fundamental to succeeding through the interview process. Other questions you might be asked are also important, but you'll need to give satisfactory answers to all three of these to be made an offer.

Draft outline responses of key points to cover in response to these questions as you prepare beforehand. Try not to memorise word for word what you'll say, but know your answers so well that when you are asked any of these questions, your response will be second nature to you.

The Three Unasked Questions

In addition to the Three Key Questions, there are another three questions that I have called the three 'unasked' questions. They are unasked because, although the interviewer won't ask you them, they are still questions the interviewer will be asking themselves *about* you. These questions are not ones that you can directly provide an answer to, but they are ones the interviewer will try to answer for themselves about you based on their experience. What does this mean? Let's take a look at the three questions to find out:

1. **Can I see myself working with this person?**
2. **Can I see my team working with this person?**
3. **Can I see this person representing us as an organisation to clients/customers?**

The interviewer can't ask you these questions because there is no response you can give that will directly satisfy the question. But the interviewer will still be asking themselves these questions. This is only relevant to the final interview. A senior person is responsible for everyone they hire, and they will only want to hire people who will fit well with the organisation, and also someone who will represent the organisation well to clients.

The first question is about establishing a rapport with your interviewer. They will not offer you a role unless they see you as someone they could work with. Showing that you are open, diplomatic, and able to be calm under pressure, rather than tense and confrontational, is important. Your interviewer might test this by asking difficult questions to put pressure on you, or pointing out something you made a mistake on. In doing so they are trying to see how open you are to criticism, how calm you remain under pressure and how receptive you are to feedback.

These are all very important elements that will help the interviewer decide whether they will be able to get on with you in a work context or not. If you become defensive and confrontational, the interviewer will not make you an offer, even if you have a lot in common. However, if you remain calm, diplomatic and appreciative of feedback, then this vastly increases the chances of you being made an offer.

Don't go too far the other way and concede or cave in when you don't need to though. The interviewer might also test whether you stand by your own answers and convictions. The approach you want is to alway be diplomatic and open to feedback, but also politely discussing through things you disagree with.

The second question revolves around your teamwork. It will largely be answered for the interviewer by both the first question (if they can see themselves working well with you, then by extension their team should work well with you. This is because employers tend to hire people who fit in with their workplace culture. If the senior interviewer is happy that they are likely to work well with you, then they will assume the same of their team) and also your performance in the group exercise (if one was included in this process). There isn't much you can directly do to influence the second question apart from performing well in your group exercise and building a good rapport with your final interviewer.

Perhaps the most important unasked question is the third one. This only applies to professional services firms, or any employer where you will be expected to represent the organisation to outside clients, customers or agencies. Here, the interviewer is assessing your professionalism.

Once an employer hires you, you become a representative of that employer *at all times.* Even if you do something foolish outside work, the chances are your actions will reflect negatively on your employer. They don't expect you to be perfect, and they certainly won't take any interest in prescribing how you act outside working hours, but they will expect you to behave with a certain level of professional dignity, etiquette and integrity.

This means that you would never do anything that would harm the reputation of the organisation or its clients. How does this translate into the interview context? Your interviewer will be asking themselves whether they can trust you to be a representative of the firm. The way they will assess this is by looking at your professionalism.

Professionalism is a term that covers a number of different behaviours. Each of these behaviours contributes to an overall view of how professional you are. For example, if you turn up to the interview late and scruffy-looking, are not polite, and are obviously eager for the interview to be over by continuously checking your watch, these behaviours contribute to the impression that you are unprofessional. Similarly, if you say negative things about other applicants, or are generally negative about other organisations or people (in an undiplomatic way), then this is also unprofessional. Professionalism really boils down to three things:

- **Empathy** (how much you consider other people): empathy is very important at work. Everyone has competing demands on their time. Being empathetic means being able to see things from another person's perspective; walking in their shoes, so to speak. So when you ask for something, you are considerate that your request is only one among a number of competing requests for that person's time. We won't look at empathy in any depth here since there isn't really any opportunity for it to become a factor during an application process. It will be very relevant once you start work however (see Section 9 The First Chapter).

- **Diplomacy** (how diplomatic you are): being diplomatic means never being overtly critical or negative about anything or anyone else. You might be saying *"never?"*. The key word at play here is 'overtly': there are ways to be negative about things. What is relevant for your interview, however, is to remember that you shouldn't speak badly of any other candidate or organisation. This will be considered unprofessional. If the interviewer goes fishing trying to get you to say something negative (e.g. "Why do you prefer our grad scheme over theirs?"), then **the trick is to be positive about both, but** *much more positive* **about this one** (e.g. "Well, on the surface both firms have good grad schemes, but your firm has a much more in-depth training programme, and you're the market leader in this field, so I definitely feel like yours is the better scheme for my development and hopefully future contribution as well").

- **Presentation** (how you present yourself): this is what comes to mind for most people when they think of professionalism. It involves your behaviours and actions. Being polite and courteous at all times, plus dressing appropriately professionally in suitable business attire.

If you follow the steps outlined so far, the interviewer should be able to make their own mind up about you, and answer the three unasked questions successfully.

Final words of advice

You are now nearing the end of your journey through the graduate application process. The following points cover some last pieces of advice for your final interview:

- **Know your application:** we saw earlier that the interviewer can ask you about any part of your application. Make sure you know your own form/CV/covering letter and what you've written on them.

- **Don't be afraid to make mistakes:** you don't need to be perfect to succeed in getting a great graduate job. Employers are not looking for the finished article, for you to be a fully trained and flawless employee of their company. They are just looking for bright and talented graduates who are humble and professional enough for them to train with the relevant technical skills so that they can *become* a great employee at their organisation. No one expects you to join a grad scheme knowing all the answers. If you make a mistake in your interview or you don't know the answer, just tell the interviewer you don't know the response to their question, but then tell them how you would go about getting the answer they want. There is no shame in admitting a mistake or that you don't know something. In fact, that's exactly what the interviewer is looking to see. They might even have asked you a difficult question to see whether you become defensive or are open and honest about your limits.

- **Always be truthful:** part of being professional is having ethical integrity at work and being honest. If you have a gap in your CV, don't be tempted to try to cover it up. Every experience has a positive side to it, even if the only positive is having learnt from the experience. Don't be tempted to be untruthful, especially about your personal details or qualifications. Not only is this unprofessional, meaning the employer will not want to hire you, but most graduate employers employ fact-checking agencies to do due diligence on you (with your permission) after they make you an offer. So the likelihood is you would be found out anyway. Also, some professions have professional bodies which take ethical integrity and honesty very seriously. Don't jeopardise your future career by not telling the truth.

- **Try not to second-guess how the interview is going:** hold back on any self-evaluation on how you think you've done until *after* the interview (and try to cut it out altogether if possible). Trying to analyse how you think it's going *during* the interview will interrupt your flow and take you out of the moment. You will come off as preoccupied and anxious rather than relaxed and interested in your discussion with the interviewer. Some interviewers have excellent 'poker faces' and are very good at not giving anything away. This might disconcert you if you think you're not building a connection with your interviewer when in fact you are. Focus on being in the moment during your interview and giving the best responses you can to the questions asked. If you make a mistake, it's fine, you're only human and the interviewer expects you to be only human; don't self-critique how you've done until afterwards.

- **Be polite, friendly and open:** being courteous and polite goes a long way to making people like you and want to work with you. But also be polite and friendly to the other candidates. Don't be afraid to make small talk with your interviewers and assessors. Let your personality shine through, let them get to know you. If you perform well during the assessment and they like you and your personality, then they'll make you an offer. It really is that simple.

PART III

OFFER STAGE AND BEYOND

8 OFFER STAGE

8.1 GETTING AN OFFER

You've just heard back from an employer and they've made you an offer. **Congratulations!!!** All of that hard work has paid off and your application journey is nearly over. But before you can completely relax, there are a few final things to consider.

Important: Grad scheme application success is *not* the same thing as simply getting onto a grad scheme. It's about getting onto the *right* grad scheme for you. Even if a prestigious employer makes you an offer, take the time to consider carefully if they are a good fit for you, and you a good fit for them. You will be saving yourself from wasting valuable time and experiencing the heartache of starting out on a path only to later realise it isn't for you. Remember that getting onto the grad scheme is just the start of your journey, and you will need to be passionate and excited about working there to succeed in the long run.

Should I accept the offer?

If you're not sure about whether you want to accept the offer, or you're in the application process for other employers and would like more time, ask what the deadline is for getting back to them on the offer. It is usually within your remit to hold off returning the signed offer for a certain period. This can be up to a few weeks, so check the offer letter, or check with your recruiter, to see how much time you have to consider the offer.

Overall, make sure you accept an offer with an employer where you can see yourself working and fitting in. If you don't fit the organisation's culture or ways of working, and it doesn't feel like a good fit for you, then don't accept an offer there. It will save you time, effort and emotional anguish, by avoiding going down the wrong road. It will also save the employer resource and finances in terms of the huge investment they put into training their graduates. Once you've decided on accepting an offer, let them know as soon as you can.

When to accept an offer

If you know that you are happy to work at this employer and are happy with the terms of the contract, you should accept. If, on the other hand, you are still in the application process for other grad schemes, then try to wait it out to see if you are successful there instead. Make sure you are conscious of the deadline for accepting your offer so that it doesn't lapse in the meantime.

But you should delay **only** if you are unsure about accepting this offer. If you know that you want to work for this employer over any others you have applied for, then sign and return the offer. Nothing would be gained from staying in the process for other employers when you have already got an offer from the one that you want. Accept the offer and graciously back out of the other applications processes to free up that space in the process for other people who want to apply.

How do I accept an offer?

You will usually be notified that you have been successful via telephone. This is then followed up by a formal offer letter. Even if you verbally accepted the offer during the telephone conversation this is not binding on you until you have signed and returned the offer letter. A contract of employment may be enclosed within the offer letter or it may follow shortly afterwards.

Make sure you wait for the contract to arrive and read through it very carefully to make sure that it is what you expect before you accept. Mistakes have been known to happen, and some candidates have even been sent the wrong contracts. Make sure the salary, benefits, and expectation for travel are all what you expect. Note that although your contractual hours may be listed as 9 to 5 or something similar, the likelihood is that you will rarely work these hours if you have applied for a professional services grad scheme. Investment banking and commercial law are known for working longer hours. Management consulting tends to be quite varied depending on project demands and deadlines but can also be very demanding and have a greater expectation around travel.

Make sure you are fully committed and happy to proceed with the grad scheme before you sign and return the contract. This contract of employment constitutes a legal document, and you cannot usually back out after you have signed it if you change your mind.

Should I try to negotiate my employment terms?

It is not advisable to try to negotiate any of the terms of your offer, unless there are very special circumstances involved. Employers usually issue a standard offer for all of their grad scheme joiners, and rarely would they make an exception for one candidate and amend any of the offer terms.

You've now reached the end of this journey and it's time to cele-
brate. Most grad schemes don't start until mid-August the
following year at the earliest, so take some time out if you can
to travel and enjoy your summer break. You're about to start a
new journey, and it'll form the start of the next phase of your
life. This is a new beginning rather than an ending, so see the
final section on 'next steps' for more on this, and how you can
really hit the ground running in your new career.

8.2 GETTING A REJECTION

I f you hear back that you haven't been successful at any stage of the process, don't let that deject you or put you off applying for other grad schemes. Like most other things in life, failure is feedback. It can only help you to improve if you learn the lessons from where you haven't been successful.

If a recruiter calls to inform you that you haven't been successful, graciously thank them for letting you know and politely ask them to provide you with feedback. They will usually have kept notes on your application, and should be able to tell you why you haven't been successful.

Ask them if they have any suggestions for improving. Knowing the reasons for this rejection will help you to know where to focus your attention on improving your application technique, and will help you to be more successful next time.

Remember to not look at this as a failure, only a temporary setback. Even better, just look at it as feedback that will help you improve as you move ever closer to your goal of landing a job on a great grad scheme.

Once you've received feedback, it's time to put that into action and get started on the next application. Think of it like a video game. When you see the 'game over' screen, just hit reset and start again; only as a more informed and even better player this time.

9 THE FIRST CHAPTER

Accepting an offer on a grad scheme or training contract is the end of one journey, and the beginning of another. Some of you, will stay on for the entirety of your grad scheme. Others, will find that this isn't for you, and move on before the scheme is over. A large number, will choose to stay on at the same employer after the grad scheme has ended. A small number, will stay at this same employer for the majority, if not all, of their careers.

Regardless of your path, know that receiving an offer to join a grad scheme is a fantastic accomplishment. The competition for these places is high. And although I firmly believe that the competition in getting a place is only with yourself rather than other candidates, being offered a place signifies something.

It signifies that you have put the hours in, that you've worked hard, and that you've gone the extra mile to get this job. These are all traits that will serve you well in the months and, hopefully, years to come. This is precisely why graduate employers make their application processes so tough. So that only people with endurance and tenacity will persevere to the end.

I hope that you will see your training contract or grad scheme through until the end. Sometimes you'll start a job only to realise that this isn't for you. Rather than going back to the drawing board, I encourage you to stay on until the completion of it. Completing a grad scheme at a graduate employer will open doors for you. Other employers, recruiters and head-hunters will come calling.

Even if you choose to completely change your career and industry after your grad scheme, the transferable skills you will have picked up will be invaluable to you in whatever endeavour or field of work you choose to pursue afterwards.

For me, having completed a grad scheme at one of the best consultancies in the world irrevocably shaped my skills, both professional and personal, for the better. What I learnt on my grad scheme laid the foundation for the rest of my career in the years that followed. I hope you will go on your own grad scheme journey and build an outstanding foundation for your career, whether you stay in the same line of work or move on afterwards.

Now that you've completed the application process and accepted an offer, you are at the start of another process. Being successful in receiving an offer does not automatically mean you will thrive on your grad scheme.

Make no mistake, a grad scheme is very hard work. It will involve lots of long hours and effort. It will require sweat and determination. It will be stressful at times and you will face setbacks. But you will also find skills and qualities in yourself that you didn't know you even had. You will also gain new skills, meet incredibly talented and intelligent people, and work at the forefront of your chosen industry.

You will develop a strong professional network and make new friends, adding to your own personal network. You will receive opportunities for your own personal and professional growth, helping push you to the next level. You may also get the opportunity to travel for work, and each day is likely to be very different from the next.

Like any journey, there will be obstacles and setbacks from time to time. Sometimes the work tasks you are given will be incredibly involving and interesting, at other times the tasks may seem dull and repetitive. I always encourage new graduates who work for me to treat their time on a grad scheme as if they are a sponge, to seek out and soak in as much information and skill from more senior and experienced team members and colleagues as they can. You will then start to build your own knowledge base and ways of working, using the best of what you have learnt from others.

Attitude is everything when you are on a grad scheme. Always keep your passion and enthusiasm for being there burning brightly and it will be reflected in the quality of your work.

This, in turn, will bring you more responsibility and promotion, faster.

I will say no more on this here, since your application journey with me is ending. I hope what you have read in these pages has been of some help in getting you the job of your dreams. If what you read in this book was useful, please rate and review; any five star reviews would be highly appreciated and greatly help this book stand out to benefit others. It will also be a confirmation to me that you have found it useful and want more like it.

Now that you have completed the application process, if you would like strategies and guidance for succeeding and excelling while **on** your grad scheme, join my mailing list to stay updated on my upcoming books on **how to excel and stand-out on your grad scheme** and also **how to achieve rapid and early promotion.**

But for now, all that is left for me to say is congratulations, and the very best of luck in your future career!

Zachary Redsmith

PLEASE LEAVE A REVIEW

If you have found this book useful it would be highly appreciated if you could please leave a rating and review.

Reviews help me gain visibility and they can bring my books to the attention of other readers who may benefit from them. They are also a helpful confirmation to me that you have found this book useful and would like further titles like it in future.

Thank you.

SPECIAL BONUS: APPLICATIONS ACCELERATOR PACK

The **Applications Accelerator Pack** is a valuable timesaver that condenses vital information, strategies and techniques you need to pass each stage of the applications process. Ideal as a refresher for the material in this book, or if you are pressed for time and would like to accelerate your preparation.

Join the Applications Fast Track mailing list to receive your **free copy**. This is a no-spam newsletter that will keep you updated on new releases from Zachary Redsmith and Careers-Geek, as well as other benefits and discounts.

It is completely free and you will never be spammed, you can opt out easily at any time.

To get your free copy of the Applications Accelerator Pack visit:
bookhip.com/CPHZST

ALSO BY ZACHARY REDSMITH

Every successful journey has a successful beginning…

Get your free copy today at:

www.careersgeek.com

ACKNOWLEDGEMENTS

— I WOULD LIKE TO THANK MY FAMILY, BOTH IMMEDIATE AND EXTENDED, FOR SHARING THE WRITING JOURNEY WITH ME, AND FOR BELIEVING. I WOULD ALSO LIKE TO THANK MY GOOD FRIENDS, TANZEED, DYLAN AND TONY, FOR THEIR UNWAVERING SUPPORT AND ENCOURAGEMENT. AND FINALLY, I WOULD LIKE TO THANK YOU, DEAR READER, I HOPE YOU FIND THIS BOOK AS USEFUL TO READ AS I DID TO WRITE.

Printed in Great Britain
by Amazon

59579775R00115